Mirko Seebeck

Wrocław
An Alternative Guide
to 100 Extraordinary Places

© 2023 by Mirko Seebeck

All rights reserved. No part of this publication may be reproduced, stored in a retrieval system, stored in a database and/or published in any form or by any means, electronic, mechanical, photocopying, recording or otherwise, without the prior written permission of the publisher. To request permission, contact the publisher at info@wroclawguide.com

Written with special credit to: Ewa Kierach

Edited by Christian A. Dumais (English Edition)
Edited by Jan W. Haas (German source text)
Final corrections by Christian A. Dumais
Cover art by Anastasia Lukina
Layout by Aleksandra Gil
Published by WroclawGuide.com, Füsilierstrasse 21, 40476 Düsseldorf, DE
Printed by Wydawnictwo Poligraf sp. z o.o., 55-093 Brzezia Łąka, PL

ISBN 978-3-9822338-4-0

Bibliographic information of the German National Library: The German National Library lists this publication in the German National Bibliography (Deutsche Nationalbibliografie); detailed bibliographic data are available on the Internet at http://dnb.dnb.de.

Prologue

Wrocław – a city full of contrasts and dramatic history. However, today it manages to captivate visitors from near and far – pretty much without exception! I might be biased but have not heard a single person who didn't like the city at all.

There's something simply magical here. Maybe it comes from the little dwarfs, which are part of the cityscape and reflect the residents in often funny ways? Or the intersection of the Polish, German, Bohemian, and Habsburg histories? Perhaps it's the water of the Oder River that flows through the city like a lifeline? Or the numerous bridges that create connections on so many levels? Or the diversity reflected in the multi-ethnic population? Or is it the contrasts that catch the eye of everyone looking through the modern, brutalist architecture of the so-called „pre-war tenement houses" clashing with the splendour of the Baroque buildings and Gothic churches? You will have to answer that for yourself.

This book will guide you through the city by stopping at one hundred (very subjective and sometimes random) extraordinary places, of which some are regularly overlooked and ignored. The German edition, the basis for this English edition, was created in the midst of the COVID pandemic and was published just as another lockdown started – certainly not the best timing from a commercial point of view. But that doesn't matter, as this book was born out of passion – it wants to pass on some enthusiasm for a unique city and therefore deliberately does it without a big publishing house that sets the tone. And with great pleasure, after a long wait, you finally have the English edition in your hands – thank you for supporting our work with your purchase!

Our city blog on WroclawGuide.com always provides the latest updates if you are looking for the most recent information. Should one of the places included in this book close or no longer be in operation, we will immediately suggest an alternative in our blog newsletter – a real guarantee of our up-to-dateness.

But now enjoy reading and exploring!

Table of Contents

1. Acoustic Mirrors on the Boulevard of Physicists 10
Oversized satellite dishes with ears

2. Bar Pierożek 12
Popular pierogi prepared with love

3. Beach Bars 14
Volleyball, yoga, and concerts in the sand

4. The Beautiful Staircases 16
Never be afraid to open some shabby doors…

5. Browar Mieszczański and the EkoBazar 18
A place for alternative events and meetings

6. Browar Stu Mostów 20
A beer with cocoa, vanilla, and tonka beans?

7. Bunker Roof Terrace 22
If you're going to a bunker, pick one with style!

8. Café Równik 24
A café with rather unusual people

9. Café Rozrusznik 26
Where the transformation of Nadodrze began

10. Cathedral Island 28
The place where it all began

11. Centennial Hall 30
A scary 5 minutes and a century of memories

12. Centennial Stones 32
Breslau or Wrocław – maybe both?

13. Charlotte 34
Probably the most popular breakfast in town

14. Cinema New Horizons 36
A cinema without popcorn?

15. City Moat (Old Town Promenade) 38
A romantic walk with culture and history

16. Cocofli 40
A bookshop with a café and wine bar attached

17. The Colourful Backyards of Nadodrze 42
Street art for real explorers

18. DIY Crucifix Kit 44
Want to be like Jesus Christ? Take the hammer...

19. The Dwarfs of Wrocław 46
A new tradition grew out of dwarf protests

20. Film Location for Bridge of Spies 48
How satellite dishes turned into good financial investments

21. Four Domes Pavilion 50
Reanimated in the year of the Capital of Culture

22. The Giant Concrete Chair 52
Out of place or exactly where it's supposed to be?

23. Gondola Bay 54
A new perspective of the city – sunburn guaranteed

24. Grunwaldzki Bridge 56
The longest suspension bridge in Poland – a prestige project

25. The Heart of Nadodrze 58
The mosaic that unites an entire neighbourhood

26. The Hidden Backyard of Gniazdo 60
A place to go not only for digital nomads

27. The Historic Market Square 62
One of the largest market squares in Europe

28. The History Trail 64
Crash course in history: Wrocław in five minutes

29. Kalambur 66
The meeting place of the artistic community

30. Kolejkowo 68
Wrocław downsized – with great attention to detail

31. Kwiaty Kawy 70
A place of well-being for all your senses

32. Leśnica Castle 72
Once burnt down by the residents of Wrocław

33. Lody Roma Ice Café 74
The first ice cream after the war – and still one of the best in town!

34. Macondo 76
Where stamp workshops meet Japanese calligraphy classes

35. Mała Czarna 78
A well-hidden local coffee roastery

36. Manhattan Building Complex 80
The city's most popular black-and-white picture spot

37. The Marina Topacz Sports Harbour 82
It doesn't have to be Saint-Tropez all the time!

38. Market Hall 84
Once upon a time, human flesh was on offer

39. Milk Bar Miś 86
The cult of cheap self-service restaurants

40. Mleczarnia 88
A rustic venue for any time: day and night

41. The Monument of Common Memory 90
Memories of the past inhabitants of Wrocław

42. The Monument of the Anonymous Pedestrians 92
One of the most creative sculptures in the world

43. The Most Beautiful Street in Wrocław 94
A beauty that comes from its normality

**44. The Museum of Games
and Computers of the Past Era** 96
From Pac-Man to the Commodore 64 to the Super Nintendo

45. The Mysterious Hand 98
No one knows where it came from

46. Nafta Neo Bistro 100
A restaurant in a former secret place

47. The Naked Swordsman 102
Somebody lost his clothes while gambling...

48. The Narrow-gauge Railway Station 104
A somewhat unusual railway station – in timber-framed style

49. The National Forum of Music 106
As long as the music is loud enough when the world ends!

50. The Nawa Sculpture 108
A dinosaur skeleton in the city centre?

51. The Neighborhood of Brochów 110
Train tracks, a maze, and tropical fruits...

52. The Neighborhood of Sępolno 112
A typical district or a big piece of art?

53. Neon Side Gallery 114
An unusual cemetery

54. The New Market Square 116
A counter-design to the Market Square and the Salt Market Square

55. The Night Market 118
When the mosquitoes buzz in summer, the Asian feeling is complete

56. The Oder River Banks 120
Why go to the seaside?

57. Odra Centrum 122
Science, a living room, and a workbench in one place

58. The Old City Port 124
A paradise for urbex photographers and Instagrammers

59. The Old Guardhouse 126
A roof terrace and the most beautiful weather station in the city

60. The Old Jewish Cemetery 128
A quiet sound in a fairytale place

61. The Old Mill Flea Market 130
Bicycle stolen? No worries, you might find it here!

62. OP ENHEIM 132
An artistic bridge between Wrocław and Berlin

63. Ossolineum Garden 134
An oasis of calm amidst the hustle and bustle of city life

64. Palace Pawłowice 136
The most beautiful arboretum in the city

65. Parrot Coffee 138
Some people bring dogs to their workplace, others bring parrots

66. Partisan Hill 140
After a long legal battle, a future is finally in sight again

67. Penitent Bridge 142
Where you end up if you just play with love…

68. Pergola and the Multimedia Fountain 144
Where light, water, and music shows meet wedding dresses

69. Polinka Cable Car 146
A cable car in the City of Bridges

70. Polish Poster Gallery 148
Why the Terminator movie poster looks different in Poland

71. Pomiędzy Café 150
In between – the translation can be taken literally

72. The Postmodernism of Wojciech Jarząbek 152
Solpol might be gone, but postmodernism still lives

73. Przedwojenna Bistro.. **154**
Creating connections with cheap beer and popular Polish snacks

74. Quarter of Four Denominations **156**
A colourful mix of religion, art, and nightlife

75. Railway Embankment (Nasyp) **158**
A pub street underneath the railway tracks

76. Renoma.. **160**
The escalators were once its biggest attraction

77. The Royal Palace (Wrocław City Museum)................ **162**
A panopticon of more than 1000 years of history

78. The Salt Market Square **164**
Flowers at any time of day or night

79. Sand Bridge and Cathedral Bridge **166**
Why criminals once appreciated Cathedral Bridge

80. Sculpture of Waiting **168**
A memorial for all those waiting

81. Słodowa Island.. **170**
Balmy summer nights on the city's most popular island

82. The Square of John Paul II **172**
A journey into the culture of underground passages

83. Stare Jatki... **174**
The miraculous transformation of mounds of meat into mounds of art

84. Świebodzki Railway Station.. **176**
From a regional train station to the place of culture

85. Szczytnicki Park and the Japanese Garden **178**
The city's largest park offers plenty of shade and tranquillity

86. Szklarnia **180**
Cocktails in a hipster greenhouse

87. Tajne Komplety.. **182**
A reminder of the times when people had to hide

88. The Traces of History in Nadodrze **184**
When the past knocks at your door

89. Traditional Pączki Pastry Shops **186**
No, pączki are not donuts! Or maybe they are?

90. The Train to Heaven... **188**
The largest urban sculpture in Poland

91. ul. Ofiar Oświęcimskich **190**
The former street of the rich and beautiful

92. The University and the Aula Leopoldina 192
One of the longest baroque facades in the world

93. Vertigo Jazz Club 194
Jazz – the favourite music of Wrocław

94. The Water Tower 196
Probably the most impressive water tower in the world

95. Wilk Syty 198
Wrocław's paradise for vegans and vegetarians

96. Wrocław Christmas Market 200
A great festival with visitors from all over the world

97. Wrocław's Main Railway Station 202
A fairytale castle or a railway station?

98. Xawery Dunikowski Promenade 204
The most beautiful views of Cathedral Island

99. Zajezdnia History Centre 206
An interactive place to understand Wrocław's post-war history

100. Zwierzyniecki Bridge 208
Fortunately, it escaped its destiny of being blown up

Bonus Chapter: What do others say? 211

City Plan 231

Picture credits 238

Big Thanks 239

Scan the QR-Code to access an interactive city map of all 100 places with zoom functionality!

Legend:

- 🎯 Address
- 🚊 Tram stop
- 🕐 Opening hours
- 🔴 Polish name
- 🌐 Internet URL
- ⏩ Suggestions on what to see next
- ❶ Hint

1. Acoustic Mirrors on the Boulevard of Physicists

Oversized satellite dishes with ears

📍 Bulwar Józefa Zwierzyckiego 🚊 Pomorska 🕐 All year round
🇵🇱 Zwierciadła akustyczne 🌐 uni.wroc.pl/zwierciadla-akustyczne-na-pocza-tek-bulwaru-fizykow ⏩ Enjoy a coffee break at Café Rozrusznik 9

Many people walk along *Bulwar Józefa Zwierzyckiego* (Zwierzycki Boulevard) without knowing that *Bulwar Fizyków* (Boulevard of Physicists) even exists. Most only notice the magnificent row of trees along the Oder River, past the State Archive, the Geological Museum, and the Faculty of Physics and Astronomy. But if they stopped, they'd most likely see the acoustic mirrors.

At first glance, the two large black objects between the trees look like giant satellite dishes. But what are they? Well, two people can talk to each other over a distance of approximately fifty metres as long as they have their backs to one another and speak directly into the mirrors. This feat was convenient during the pandemic when it was possible to have a joyful conversation between friends without violating distancing rules.

This installation was created by lecturers and students at the Faculty of Physics and Astronomy to redesign and reanimate the area and rescue it from falling into oblivion. And it's only the beginning! Soon there will be an extensive physics garden, a sundial, some optical illusions, and other experimental objects. There is also a design for an amphitheatre that will make outdoor lectures accessible to everyone.

What comes next depends on the citizens of Wrocław, more specifically, the *Wrocławski Budżet Obywatelski* (Wrocław Citizens' Budget). This exciting concept lets all citizens directly decide by vote which public projects to finance with their taxes. In 2020, the available budget was 25 million Polish zloty.

2 Bar Pierożek

Popular pierogi prepared with love

📍 E

📍 Księcia Józefa Poniatowskiego 3 🚋 Na Szańcach 🕐 Mon–Fri 10–19h, Sat 10–16h 🍴 Bar Pierożek 🌐 barpierozek.wroclaw.pl/menu ⏭ A sweet dessert and some parrots are waiting for you across the street at Parrot Coffee **65**!

What would a visit to Poland be without pierogi? The popular Polish dumplings can be found on almost every street corner in Wrocław, but the best ones are hidden north of the city centre. At Bar Pierożek, you won't just see workers from the surrounding offices meeting for lunch, but people from all social backgrounds - construction workers dining with students, corporate workers sharing tables with neighbourhood residents.

During the summer, the takeaway option is preferred, as one of the most popular hangout destinations, *Wyspa Słodowa* (Słodowa Island), is only a few minutes walk away. Pierogi is a typical Polish dish with various fillings, such as meat, cabbage and mushrooms, and spinach. The classic option is *pierogi ruskie* which are filled with potatoes and cottage cheese and often come with pan-fried onions or sour cream. If you want something sweeter, try pierogi with strawberries, blueberries, or cherries – as a dessert or main course. Ordering different styles and sharing is a good idea when visiting with a group.

There are many so-called *pierogarnia* in Wrocław – most located around the market square – and it's worth noting that the pierogi tends to be overpriced and of low quality. Bar Pierożek is a highly recommended alternative as the prices are reasonable since most tourists have yet to discover this hidden gem. The décor is minimalistic, as Bar Pierożek focuses on the pierogi itself. The dough and filling are prepared – as well as the shaping of the pierogi – on the spot.

By the way, a little advice if you would like to order your pierogi properly. Pierogi is already the plural version and the word „pierogis" doesn't exist – the singular version in Polish would be „pieróg". But honestly, who would order just one?

3 Beach Bars

📍 E,F

Volleyball, yoga, and concerts in the sand

Stara Odra Beach Bar 🚋 Zawalna 53 🚌 Trzebnicka,
Basen Beach Bar 🚋 Pasterska 🚌 Trzebnicka,
ZaZoo Beach Bar 🚋 Wybrzeże Wyspiańskiego 39E 🚌 Hala Stulecia
🌐 https://www.wroclawguide.com/en/the-best-beach-bars-in-wroclaw/
🕐 May to September ❱❱ Have a walk along the banks of the Oder River **56**

When planning a trip, you might consider whether you want to visit a city or take a beach holiday. The good news is that you can do both in Wrocław. With the Oder River and its tributaries flowing through Wrocław like a lifeline, it seems only logical that there would be beaches, right?

Despite the beach bars in Wrocław having artificial tropical decor and sand delivered, guests can get close to the feeling of a beach holiday. Outside of the cool drinks, many beach bars offer free concerts, yoga classes, volleyball, and relaxing electronic music.

And, of course, there is an army of street food trucks ready and waiting for hungry people. Many successful Wrocław restaurants started out by operating such trucks next to beach bars. The local foodie scene accepts these innovative newcomers with open arms.

Unfortunately, only one thing prevents you from having an authentic beach holiday experience: you can not legally get into swimwear and jump into the Oder. Stand-up paddling is a good alternative, and if you can't maintain your balance, you'll at least have an excellent excuse to enjoy the Oder's cool water. It is said that some beach bar visitors have „accidentally" fallen into the river after drinking too much alcohol…

In the northern part of the city, there are plenty of beach bars perfectly ideal for evening beach bar hopping. The ZaZoo Beach Bar is near the Centennial Hall, the Four Domes Pavilion, and – you guessed it – Wrocław Zoo. So if you want to rest between these mentioned sightseeing points, this is the place.

4 The Beautiful Staircases

Never be afraid to open some shabby doors…

C,D

- see text for individual locations and accessibility
- Renoma for *Plac Teatralny 1* and *Podwale 37/38*
- Piękne klatki schodowe ▶▶ The backyard of Gniazdo **26**

A lot of surprises might be waiting for you behind closed doors. In Wrocław, you can still find some old tenement houses where the paint is crumbling and most people would refer to these buildings as "renovation-worthy". But don't get fooled based on first impressions. Be brave enough to open some of these doors and you might find beautiful things you would not have expected…

Let's take the example of the office building located at ul. Wita Stwosza 16, just sneak in and you actually can find one of the prettiest staircases in Wrocław. Its shape resembles the perfect geometrical golden spiral which makes it one of the most aesthetic shapes to see in the city. This example, however, is one of the easiest to access. If you like it and want more, you'll have to put some effort into it.

Taking another beautiful example of a beautiful staircase located at Plac Teatralny 1 with ornaments in the handrails, combined with a chess-inspired black and white tiled floor. Unfortunately, you can't simply walk in and start a photo session. The main door is mostly closed, so either you are happy to have a sneak peek through the backyard of Gniazdo, or get creative. People sometimes just wait for somebody to enter or leave and then take advantage of the small window of opportunity to get inside. Other people ring the doorbell and announce themselves as parcel drivers to get in. This is not a recommendation – just a description of what people are willing to do to get in :)

A third option comes with another catch. This one is located in the little shopping center at Podwale 37/38. You can easily access the old staircase which wraps around an open steel elevator, and many beautiful Art Deco elements can be discovered there. Unfortunately, it seems that they have had enough of photo tourism, so there are little signs prohibiting photography. But honestly, these signs are very small, and it is easy to overlook them… ;)

Not a fan of staircases? No problem. There are hidden doors, like the one at ul. Kazimierza Jagiellończyka 32. When you open it, you'll discover impressive ceiling decorations. Though, they require renovation…

5 Browar Mieszczański and the EkoBazar

A place for alternative events and meetings

🚩 Hubska 44 – 48   🚌 Hubska (Dawida)   🕐 EkoBazar: Sat 8–15h   🍺 Browar Mieszczański   🌐 ekobazarwroclaw.com   » Check out Kolejkowo **30**

In the beautiful red brick buildings and courtyards of the former *Browar Mieszczański* (Mieszczański brewery), there is little left to remind you of the brewers who once worked there. Instead, the brewery has become one of the most popular meeting places for Wrocław's alternative and ecological scene.

Numerous colourful events regularly take place there, such as the Street Food Festival, which enriches Wrocław with local cuisine from all over the world, and the popular Coffee Festival. Foodies will think they're in paradise, but it's not just the culinary scene that is well represented: artistic workshops are available for photographers, jewelry makers, designers, or gardeners.

Even the alternative theatre, *Teatr Ad Spectatores*, is there. At one of the highly experimental performances, the audience is picked up in the city, blindfolded, and taken to an unknown location where they are now part of the play – as corpses.

If you're looking for something a little less adventurous, you'll appreciate the EkoBazar as a calmer alternative. Every Saturday between 8 am and 3 pm, small and local farms and shops offer their goods, and you will find all the ingredients you'll need for a healthy lifestyle. People know each other there, so the whole bazaar is reminiscent of a cosy family reunion. The Syrian breakfast available there is a must for every visitor to Wrocław.

In addition, the EkoBazar is a good starting point for market-hopping, as the *Wrocławski Bazar Smakoszy*, a similar weekend market, is just a brisk five-minute walk away at ul. Paczkowska 26.

6 Browar Stu Mostów

A,D *A beer with cocoa, vanilla, and tonka beans?*

📍 Jana Długosza 2 🚊 Kromera 🕐 Daily 14 – 0h 🍺 Browar Stu Mostów 🌐 100mostow.pl » Those who don't want to go home yet can continue in the Quarter of Four Denominations 74

Even though Wrocław has changed significantly in recent decades, the love for good beer remains the city's trademark. Even in pre-war times, there used to be around twenty breweries in the city with centuries of brewing tradition. As with other countries, however, the Polish beer market has been undergoing a process of concentration – the three largest breweries in Poland now have a market share of around eighty percent, and the growth of mass breweries seems unstoppable.

But the small, often owner-operated microbreweries are experiencing a high influx simultaneously – and with it, the craft beer scene. *Browar Stu Mostów* (Brewery of a Hundred Bridges) is an exciting example of a highly successful craft beer microbrewery. It has many unique and experimental creations, such as the Tonka, Vanilla, and Chocolate Baltic Porter Nitro – a dark beer with notes of cocoa, vanilla, and tonka beans. But don't worry, even ordinary beers like classic pilsners are brewed freshly with a lot of love and heart.

Of course, you can taste all the varieties in the brewing room. The adjoining pub is next to the brewing kettles, where guests can watch the brewing process from a gallery. In addition to the brewery's specialties, there is a vast selection of guest beers.

Browar Stu Mostów has not only established itself as a recognised member of the local and regional brewing scene, but the creations of the young Wrocław brewery are also famous on the international stage.

In the summer, the inner courtyard is transformed into a beer garden and attracts many cyclists and walkers out on the banks of the Oder who want to make a little stop. The food prepared here, by the way, has little in common with typical brewery cuisine. Instead of enormous pork knuckles with fries and ketchup, the menu features a variety of creative dishes paired with the beers on offer.

For those, who won't manage the way up north, check out their city centre pub at ul. Świdnicka 4!

7 Bunker Roof Terrace

If you're going to a bunker, pick one with style!

🗺 A

- -

📍 Plac Strzegomski 2a 🚊 Plac Strzegomski (Muzeum Współczesne)
🕐 Wed–Sun 12–20h, Mon 10–18h ⛔ Muzeum Współczesne
🌐 muzeumwspolczesne.pl » Naturally, you'll have to enjoy the view of the Train to Heaven **90**

- -

Who would have thought what you could do with former German air raid shelters? During the Second World War, between 1940-1943, five bunkers were constructed in Wrocław: on Plac Strzegomski, ul. Stalowa, ul. Ładna, ul. Ołbińska, and ul. Białodrzewna. For this entry, we'll be focusing on the bunker on Plac Strzegomski.

It was initially built in the pleasant style of late Classicism to distract from its actual purpose – protecting people from bombs. Perhaps this is why it is not immediately apparent that the reinforced concrete walls are 110 centimetres thick.

The structure was more or less left to decay for decades until a group of illegal squatters chose the bunker as their new home. In the late 1990s, it was used as a storage and business space, and there was even a pub. After some renovation work in 2011, it became *Muzeum Współczesne Wrocław* (Wrocław Contemporary Museum) – a museum with controversial contemporary art at times.

Even if you don't want to buy a ticket for the museum, you can take the lift in the middle of the former bunker to get up to the sixth floor. This is where the hidden gem, the roof terrace café, is located at a height of 25 metres.

The view quickly reveals which of the surrounding areas were heavily destroyed during the war – you'll see huge Soviet-style apartment blocks instead. A vivid contrast is provided by the iconic buildings of Wrocław's skyline on the horizon, including Sky Tower. The roofs of the main churches are also relatively easy to identify from there.

The rooftop terrace café provides an unusual outdoor setting to read a book or simply take a rest. In bad weather, you can make yourself comfortable in the winter garden with ceiling-high glass windows and enjoy the view of the city from another perspective.

8 Café Równik

A café with rather unusual people

📍 E

📍 Jedności Narodowej 47 🚇 Paulińska 🕐 Tue–Sun 11–20h
⊖ Cafe Równik 🌐 caferownik.pl » Have a little walk around the Marina Topacz Sports Harbour **37**

Wrocław has hundreds of cafés, each with its own charm. Since 2018, *Café Równik* (Equator Café) has had an exceptional and unique selling point – its staff.

People with exceptional backgrounds work here, such as those with autism and mental illnesses. However, the staff has made such good progress in their treatment that they can communicate without difficulty and pursue regular work. These people, unfortunately, are often on the edges of society, but here they are fully integrated into everyday life. And in the event of a difficult situation, therapists are available on-site for support. They often receive great feedback in their conversations with the guests, which also positively impacts their condition in many ways.

Above all, the staff implements the gastronomic vision of hospitality with heart and soul, with a passion that other places often lack. For example, English or German is spoken with lots of enthusiasm, and help is gladly provided for visitors who do not speak Polish.

Are there downsides? Well, you may get disciplined when you try to return dishes – after all, that is the server's job, and you should leave the dishes for them. And unfortunately, sometimes there are incomprehensible online reviews, such as the one about the server who ran away without a word after being asked about the selection of cakes (it turned out that he only went to the kitchen to check the available options quickly). Therefore, one should have a fundamental empathy for the concept before enjoying this unique experience!

It's worth noting that this project has even received an award from the Polish president.

9 Café Rozrusznik

Where the transformation of Nadodrze began

📍 E

📍 Wojciecha Cybulskiego 15 🚇 Pomorska 🕐 Mon–Fri 7:30–20h, Sat–Sun 10–20h ⊙ Cafe Rozrusznik 🌐 facebook.com/caferozrusznik

» Visit the film locations from *Bridge of Spies* **20**

Perhaps somewhat hidden at first glance, the small Café Rozrusznik is just a few minutes from the city centre.

The name is especially apt, as *rozrusznik* (starter – as in a car engine) could also reflect the café being the starting point of the transition from the formerly shady Nadodrze neighbourhood and is therefore closely linked to its development. The courage and confidence in opening such a café in a rather dubious area, especially back then, cannot be overstated. Fortunately, the bravery paid off at the end of the day because not only did the café prove to be a complete success, but the opening triggered a natural chain reaction, as many entrepreneurs followed Café Rozrusznik's example and opened small shops, cafés, and restaurants in the area.

In just a few years, Nadodrze has become a popular art district, and apart from a few slightly tipsy figures staggering through the parks even in the early afternoon, there are hardly any dangers left.

Today, the area is often compared to Berlin-Kreuzberg – the similarities are undeniable. Vintage lovers will get their money's worth at Café Rozrusznik: the interior is kept in a cosy vintage style and exudes a great living room atmosphere. On busy days, you can just hide somewhere among the many green plants inside, while in the summer, the colourful wooden construction that serves as a terrace invites you to watch what's happening outside. As for the coffee, those who appreciate particularly exquisite coffee beans will be happy, as well as the numerous specialty coffee brewing methods on offer.

Recently, there have been pop-up breakfasts on some Sundays, where different guest chefs prepare a small but specific and unusual breakfast menu for visitors thirsty for coffee.

One last thing: Be sure to take a look up at the building! You'll find a particular mural that interacts with its inhabitants through the lights and windows.

10 Cathedral Island
The place where it all began

E

● Ostrów Tumski ● Plac Bema ● All year round ● Ostrów Tumski
● Get to another panoramic point and check out how the city looks from the Penitent Bridge 67

The history of Wrocław began in this magical place. As early as the 9th century, the Slavic tribe of the Silesians settled here. In the early 10th century, Silesia was under Bohemian rule. It was most likely the Czech prince Vratislav (ruling from 914-921) who built the castle complex called Vratislavia and gave the city its name.

After the late 10th-century conquest by the Polish Piast Duke Mieszko I, the diocese of Wrocław was finally founded in the year 1000 in the so-called „Act of Gniezno" – the first written mention of the city.

Today, many visitors consider Cathedral Island the most beautiful part of the city, and is home to Wrocław's oldest churches. First and foremost is St. Giles' Church from the 13th century, which is not only the oldest in the city but also the oldest building in Wrocław that is still completely preserved.

One of the city's prominent landmarks, the towers of the Cathedral of St. John the Baptist, proudly makes an appearance over Cathedral Island at a height of almost 98 metres. The construction officially began in 1158, although evidence of the Piast's first work with wooden construction elements dates back to years earlier. The construction period is estimated at approximately 500 years, during which time there were repeated extensions, alterations, and a couple of destructions. The tower's spires, visible from most of the city today, were not put back until 1991. The photographs at the bottom of the cathedral are awe-inspiring, which show its dramatic destruction during the Second World War.

Cathedral Island is undoubtedly a tourist hotspot and one of the most photographed motifs in the city – rightly so, of course. Cars are not allowed there, except for the small electric vehicles used for guided city tours. At sunset, another remarkable spectacle awaits visitors: the gas lanterns are lit by hand as tradition. And so the lantern lighter in the black robe (who would have thought that this job still exists?) is also captured in many pictures.

11 Centennial Hall

A scary 5 minutes and a century of memories

📍 F

🚇 Wystawowa 1 🚊 Hala Stulecia 🕐 All year round 🛑 Hala Stulecia
🌐 halastulecia.pl ⟫ Visit the most beautiful street in Wrocław **43**

Designed by Max Berg with inspiration from the Pantheon in Rome, the Centennial Hall *(Hala Stulecia)* was a record holder during its 1913 inauguration. It was the largest reinforced concrete building in the world – the dome alone had a free span of 65 metres in diameter. Because of this, numerous sceptics believed the construction would collapse within 5 minutes after removing the concrete support.

You can imagine how nervous the construction team must have been on the day of completion. Even the frightened workers refused to remove the formwork from the concrete pillars. Finally, Max Berg himself had to persuade a random pedestrian to do it – a gold coin is said to have helped. The fact that Berg didn't want to do it himself speaks volumes.

The hall was also the home of an organ from the workshop of the famous Frankfurt organ builder Wilhelm Sauer. With 15,133 pipes and 200 organ registers, it was the largest organ in the world at the time. After the war, the organ was dismantled. Most of its components currently make up the largest organ in Poland, which you can see at the Cathedral of St. John the Baptist in Wrocław.

Surprisingly, the monumental hall managed to survive the war mostly undamaged. It was renamed the People's Hall *(Hala Ludowa)* and used as a cinema in the 1970s and 1980s. A general renovation was carried out for Pope John Paul II's visit to Wrocław in 1997. Today, it is a trendy venue for fairs and concerts.

In 2006, UNESCO designated the building a World Cultural Heritage Site, although the original 1913 design had to be completely restored.

Since its subsequent renovation in 2010, the hall has been operating under its original name – as given on the occasion of the Centennial Exhibition in 1913 to mark the centenary of the Battle of Leipzig.

Since it's been over 100 years since its completion, we think it's safe to say the sceptics were wrong.

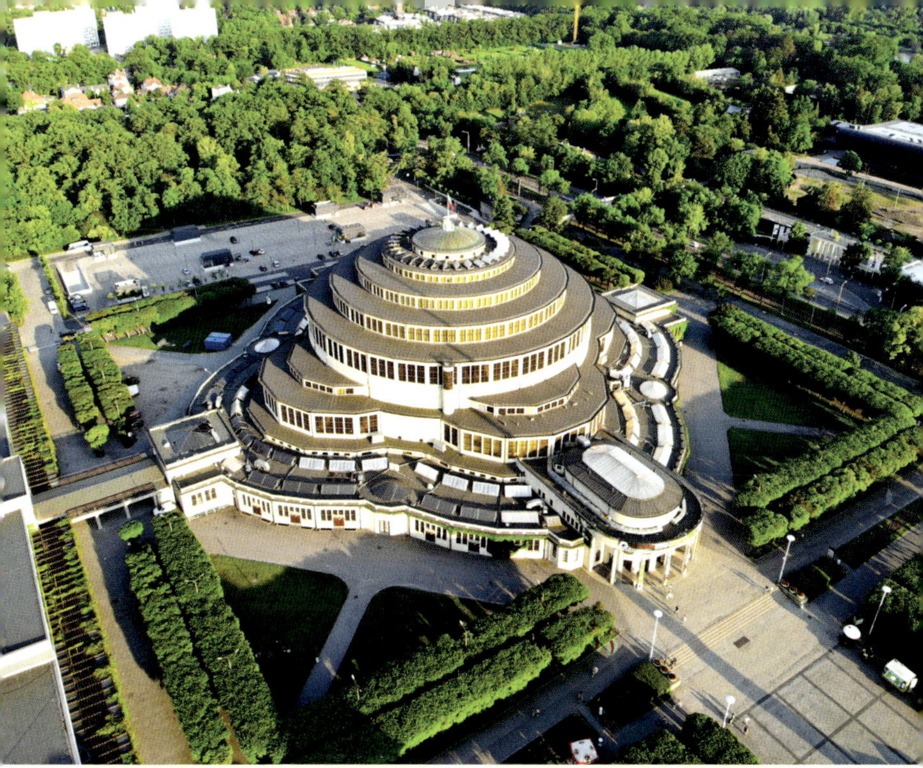

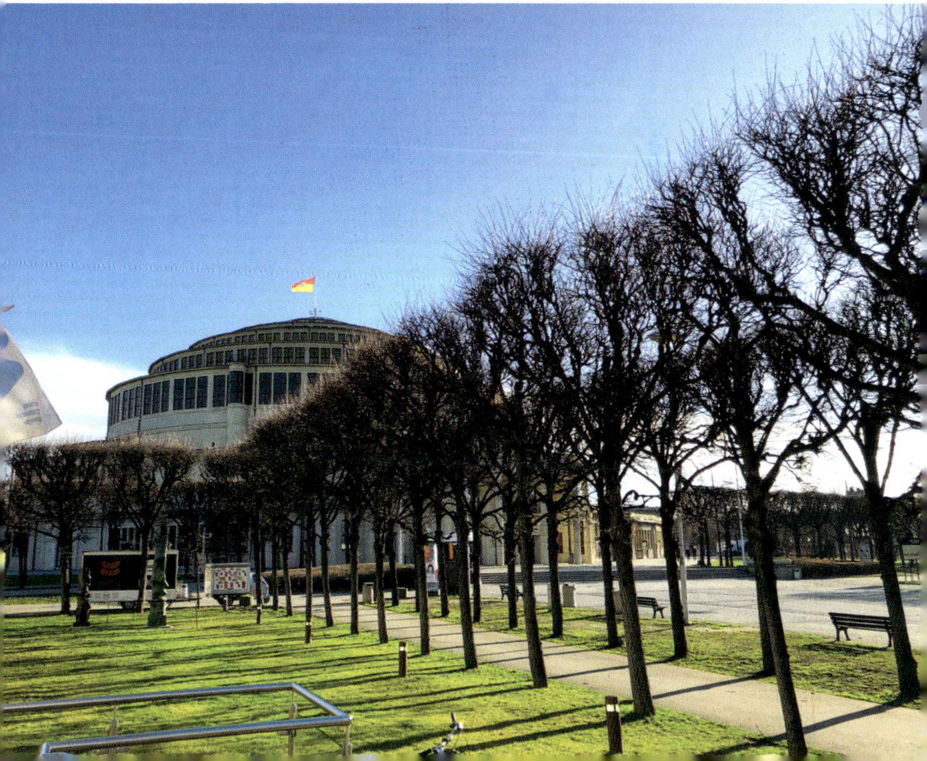

12 Centennial Stones

Breslau or Wrocław – maybe both?

A,B,E

🚊 Na Polance 5 (North), Adama Mickiewicza 91 (East), Aleja Karkonoska 8 (South) 🚌 Broniewskiego (North), Sępolno (East), Krzyki (South) 🕐 All year round 🛑 Słup graniczny miasta Wrocław ➡️ See the southern stone at the end and check out the most beautiful water tower right after **94**

On three of Wrocław's arterial roads, you'll find peculiar granite pillars with the inscription „Gemarkung Breslau" or „Gemarkung Wrocław" – but what is this all about?

At the turn of the 20th century, the so-called „Centennial Stones" were erected on the then-city border. Although the border posts never fulfilled any actual function, their shape is reminiscent of traditional Silesian border signs from the 16th century.

The round pillars designed by Karl Klimm bear not only the German name of the town (*Breslau*) but also the date of construction and the elements of the town's coat of arms from 1530 – John the Baptist as the patron saint of the Wrocław Cathedral, the Silesian eagle with a cross on its breast, the Bohemian lion, the letter W for the city's founder Wratislaw, and the golden-haloed head of John the Evangelist. Since 1990, this coat of arms has been officially used again.

Out of the former six Centennial Stones, three are still preserved. On one of the remaining stones, "Breslau" was replaced by "Wrocław" after the Second World War, which in association with the year 1901, is meant to be appreciated with a certain sense of humour. Especially since the other two still carry the original name today.

The Centennial Stones represent an inconsistent and controversial approach to the city's German past. You can also find this in other areas: the destruction of German traces, Polonisation, indifference, and deliberate preservation.

Hints of the past lurk on almost every corner of the city, as do the Centennial Stones, which is why Wrocław is so interesting from a historical point of view.

13 Charlotte

Probably the most popular breakfast in town

C

📍 Świętego Antoniego 2/4 🚌 Narodowe Forum Muzyki 🕐 Mon–Thu 7–0h, Fri 7–1h, Sat 8–1h, Sun 8–22h 🇵🇱 Charlotte 🌐 bistrocharlotte.pl ⏩ Explore the Neighborhood of Sępolno and then WuWa just a bit further out **52**

Who hasn't experienced this? You returned home a little later than you intended last night, and now your eyes won't open all the way. Don't worry; professional help is available – with a choice of prosecco or strong coffee.

In the heart of the neighbourhood of Four Denominations, Charlotte is the city's breakfast paradise. As soon as you enter the newly renovated Pokoyhof – a courtyard better known as a party scene – the smell of freshly baked bread will greet you like a warm hug.

Inspired by French pastry shops, you'll find classic baked bread and delicious and sweet pastries. But it isn't just the baked goods that make the café so popular with Wrocław residents: in the classic breakfast basket, you'll find homemade jams or chocolate spreads. Since the choice can sometimes be difficult, the white chocolate cream is highly recommended. If you don't want to try everything on the spot, you can buy some bread and its spreads to take away.

The change of scenery that takes place over the day is also exciting. As soon as the last breakfast guests have been served in the late afternoon, Charlotte – inspired by French bistros – transforms into a great wine bar! What could be better than enjoying a glass of wine in the sunshine in one of Wrocław's best-renovated courtyards?

A word of advice: as the weekend crowds are pretty big, don't arrive too late for breakfast, or there'll be a bit of a waiting time.

14 Cinema New Horizons
A cinema without popcorn?

📍 C

📍 Kazimierza Wielkiego 19a/21 🚊 Rynek 🕐 All year round
🇵🇱 Kino Nowe Horyzonty 🌐 kinonh.pl
»» Discuss the movie over a glass of wine at Cocofli **16**

When you think of cinema, popcorn almost always comes to mind. In this sense, *Kino Nowe Horyzonty* (Cinema New Horizons) is not a cinema. It's a cultural meeting space with a couple of movie theatres as a side business.

Founded in 2012 with the city's support, it is now one of the largest alternative cinemas in Europe. But as already indicated, the focus here is not only on movies but on cinematography as a whole. Famous filmmakers regularly come here to have discussions with the audience, answer questions, and give fascinating insights into their work.

Outside the film and event programme, the cinema is also popular as a meeting place and café. So it's not uncommon to see groups of visitors playing board games, musicians trying their hand at the piano, digital nomads working out of the cinema's „living room," and art lovers. In the small alternative shop, you can find books, old film posters, and attractive postcards designed by Polish artists. In any case, it's a worthwhile and inexpensive alternative to the souvenirs available around the Market Square or the Christmas Market. The regular film festivals are notable highlights: tickets for the American Film Festival or German Weeks are usually sold out immediately.

Even without knowing the Polish language, a visit is worthwhile: most movies are shown in the original language, very often in English with Polish subtitles. Polish films, on the other hand, are often shown with English subtitles. For expats in Wrocław, there is also the "Polish Cinema for Beginners" series.

So all visitors get their money's worth here – including families, for whom there are separate screenings where no one has to apologise for noisy children. Even yoga classes are offered directly in front of the screen.

15 City Moat
C,D (Old Town Promenade)

A romantic walk with culture and history

- Podwale Plac Jana Pawła II (Starting the walk counterclockwise)
- All year round Promenada Staromiejska Stop at the old guardhouse for a coffee or ice cream to go **59** Inside Park Staromiejski, close to Renoma, you'll find a beautiful old carousel

The city fortifications built in the 13th century once marked the borders of Wrocław, as a complex defence system surrounded the city at the time. However, this could not prevent Napoleon's troops from invading and conquering the city in 1807. While the fortifications were later demolished, their locations are still clearly visible on city maps, such as the ring road *Podwale* (city moat).

The nearly three-kilometre-long walk along the so-called *Promenada Staromiejska* (Old Town Promenade) exudes an enchanting atmosphere in many places. Numerous park benches invite you to admire the green surroundings. In the summer, young couples often enjoy themselves away from parental supervision.

There are numerous sights along the promenade, including various sculptures for a more artistic touch. Suppose you start your walk in the western part of the city in a counterclockwise direction. In that case, you will reach the newly-built National Forum of Music shortly after the Quarter of Four Denominations, located directly on the moat's edge. Further along the path, you will pass impressive buildings such as the City Court or the police headquarters and Partisan Hill – formerly one of the city's most popular recreation spots.

You can enjoy great water views at the floating restaurant Domek nad Fosą. Many years ago, it was possible to rent gondolas here to float across the water on your own – rumour has it that this attraction will be offered again in the future.

On the last stretch of the path, just before the Galeria Dominikanska shopping centre, the German General Consulate is in a magnificent villa. At the northeastern end of the Old Town Promenade, where it finally meets the Oder River, the remains of the former fortification can still be seen at an old bastion.

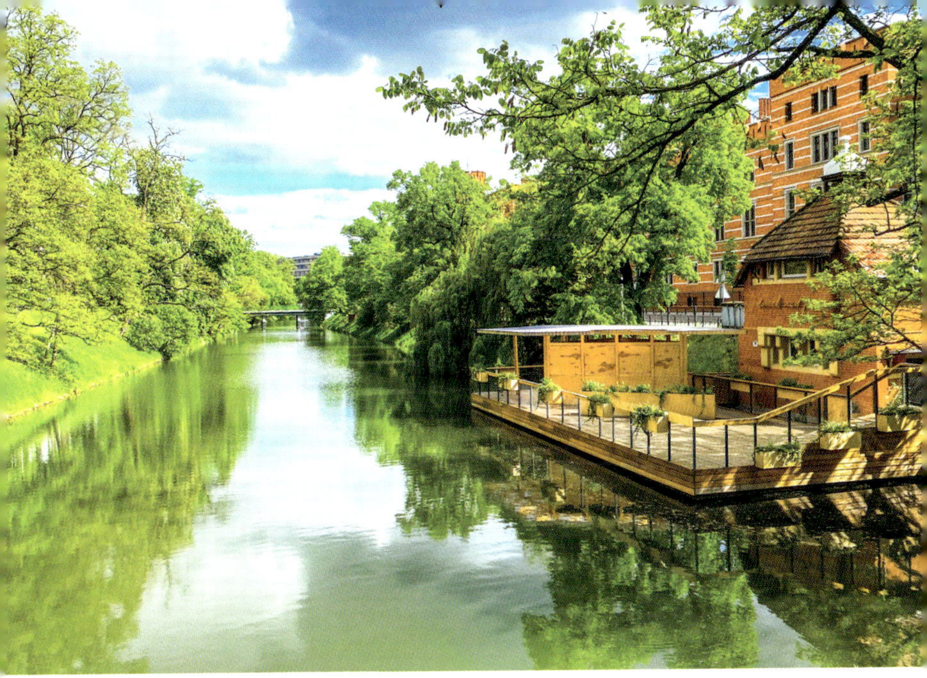
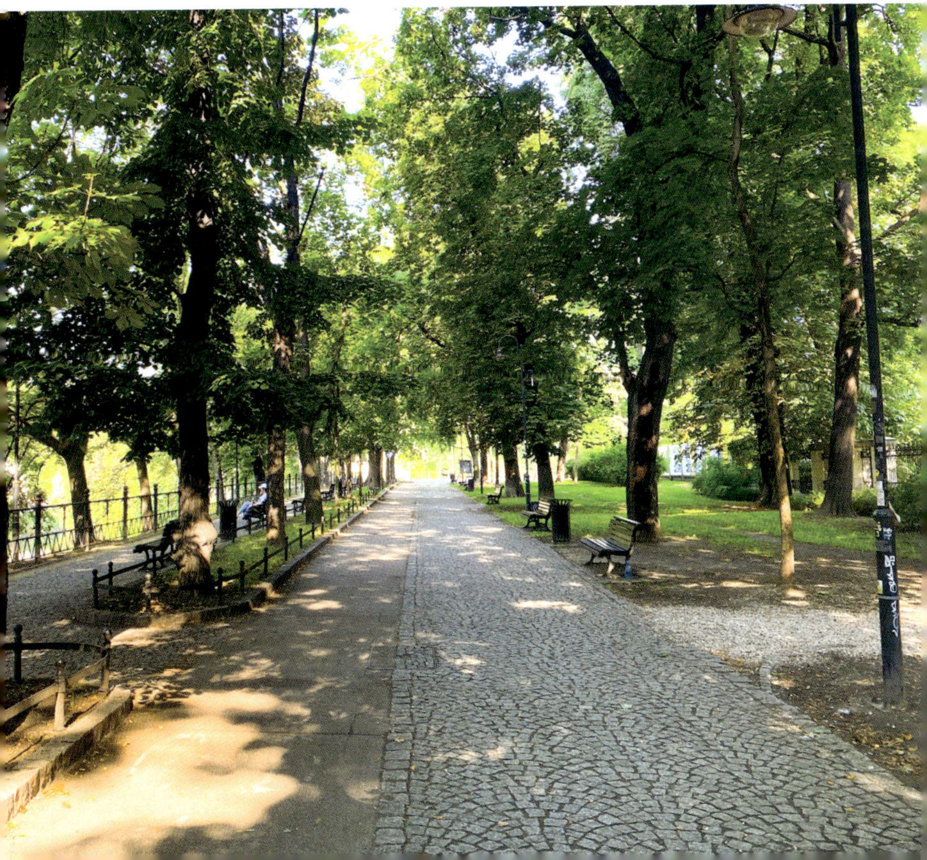

16 Cocofli

A bookshop with a café and wine bar attached

C

- Pawła Włodkowica 9 Narodowe Forum Muzyki
- Daily 12–22h, Fri+Sat until 0h Cocofli
- cocofli.pl » Move on to the night market during the summer season 55

If you're missing your own four walls while travelling or just craving a cosy sofa to read a book in candlelight, you will feel at home at Cocofli. And that's even though, at first glance, it's not entirely clear what Cocofli actually is.

During the day, you'll find a small café with the usual coffee-making utensils, such as an AeroPress, Chemex, or V60. Not entirely coincidentally, a small bookshop is integrated into the café.

It's not easy to tell which of the two parts is the main business, but as the evening progresses, it becomes a little more surprising. As night falls, the room begins to fill with romantic candlelight, and the mixture of hipster café and bookshop transforms into something magical: one of the most beautiful wine bars in Wrocław. This is when couples and groups of friends wanting to start their night out with a good glass of wine are more likely to appear. You'll also find delicious chocolate truffles offered on the side – a specialty of the house that nobody should refuse to try.

No matter how Cocofli presents itself, whether as a café, bookshop, or wine bar, it is a place of well-being at any time of the day. Cocofli is in the middle of the Quarter of Four Denominations and offers numerous options for going out later in the evening – either to one of the clubs around the Niepolda passage or Pokoyhof or simply to some of the many pubs and bars just around the corner.

There is a huge selection of highly-recommended regional Polish wines available as well. Maybe your next holiday will include some winery-hopping in Lower Silesia?

17 The Colourful Backyards of Nadodrze

Street art for real explorers

📍 Franklina Delano Roosevelta 14–16 🚊 Słowiańska 🕐 All year round
🌐 Kolorowe Podwórka na Nadodrzu 🌐 facebook.com/OsrodekKulturalnejAnimacjiPodworkwej ›› Use this area as a starting point to explore the Traces of History in Nadodrze 88.

At first glance, ul. Franklina Delano Roosevelta appears to be quite average. However, attentive explorers will notice the creatively designed driveways when going a bit further.

There are shelves on the walls and, for example, a desk has been firmly anchored to the wall – apparently dedicated to the famous painter Van Gogh. This installation, however, only marks the beginning of the colourful backyards on this street.

As soon as you pass through one of the driveways, the actual dimensions open up: for about 250 metres, there are vibrant murals and graffiti, as well as sculptures and other artistic creations made from all kinds of materials. In a +1,200 square metre area, a dreary inner courtyard in a prefabricated building style has been transformed into a work of art.

What is notable is that this was done by the residents. Almost all of them actively participated in the design. On many walls, you can find paintings of pets, such as dogs and cats, which are probably roaming around in front of the mural. And the residents and their hobbies are immortalized on the walls; so who knows, maybe the gentleman from the graffiti will suddenly appear and stand next to it?

Even the German filmmaker Wim Wenders was enthusiastic about the creatively designed backyards when he attended the European Film Festival in Wrocław.

The audio walks of Łokietka 5 – the information point for Nadodrze – are also highly recommended for those interested in street art. They lead through the district and offer exciting insights into the stories and places that would otherwise be overlooked.

> Only a few minutes away you can admire the beautiful building of the Faculty of Architecture (at Bolesława Prusa 53/55), together with a beautiful park.

18 DIY Crucifix Kit

*Want to be like Jesus Christ?
Take the hammer...*

🕀 Świętego Mikołaja 1 🚌 Rynek 🕐 All year round 🇵🇱 Krzyż Zrób to sam
⏩ Just opposite, you'll find the Przedwojenna Bistro for beers and traditional Polish snacks **73**

The German writer Wiglaf Droste once wrote, „Do you want to be like Jesus Christ? Take the hammer, and then you will be!" Theoretically, he could have met the Polish artist Eugeniusz Get-Stankiewicz. Even though it probably never happened, there seems to be a connection between the two personalities.

Another coincidence is that Get-Stankiewicz lived in the beautiful *Kamienice Jaś i Małgosia* (Hansel and Gretel house) right next to the vast St. Elizabeth's Church with the highest Gothic tower in the country. And perhaps it was precisely this circumstance that provided the decisive impetus for his controversial art installation in the traditionally very-Catholic Poland.

We are talking about a crucifix in which Jesus Christ is not already hanging on the cross and suffering but has to be taken there first by the observer. The figure is somewhat out of place to the left of the cross. On the right side of the cross, a hammer and three nails invite you to take action.

According to the legend, the artist got the idea while visiting a factory that manufactured religious products and where, among other things, figures of Jesus were continually nailed to crosses. There is no official explanation – the interpretation of the artwork is up to the audience. And there has been no recorded reaction from the church opposite.

In 1977, when the sculpture was installed, the artist thought of his international audience and kindly translated the imperative „*Zrób to Sam*" (Do it yourself) into English. However, no one seems to have heard the call so far – the hammer and nails are still next to the cross. Maybe it's because the installation is placed a little higher. Or perhaps it's because many Poles are still very religious.

19 The Dwarfs of Wrocław

📍 All

A new tradition grew out of dwarf protests

🚇 All over the city 🕐 All year round 🇵🇱 Krasnale 🌐 krasnale.pl
» Café Rozrusznik is dwarf-free so far… **9**?

The dwarf hunt in Wrocław is undoubtedly one of the most popular activities for visitors from all over the world. But how did it come about that the entire city is now virtually taken over by the little dwarf figures?

It started with a political protest in the 1980s – the so-called „Orange Alternative" movement – to show dissatisfaction with the communist regime. It is well-known how the communist government usually dealt with critics and how dangerous it could be to express an opinion that differed from the official line.

For example, anti-communist graffiti was regularly painted over so that its unwanted message was no longer visible. Starting in August 1982, members of the movement began painting pictures of dwarfs over the painted-over graffiti. Because wouldn't it be ridiculous if the government censored murals of dwarfs?

Over time, the colour orange crystallised as a response to communist red, and at protest events, participants began to wear orange headgear reminiscent of gnome caps.

Thus the „Dwarf Uprising of Wrocław" became a silent but obvious form of protest. At that time, however, there were no bronze statues – their invasion began in June 2001 at ul. Świdnicka when *Papa Krasnal* (Papa Dwarf), a commemorative figure of the protests at that time, was erected. This triggered an avalanche of unexpected proportions. In 2005, another five dwarfs were erected in the city, all designed by the artist Tomasz Moczek. Since then, the dwarfs have miraculously multiplied almost exponentially; by now, every conceivable variation can be found. There is a dwarf orchestra, a prison dwarf, a selfie dwarf, a computer dwarf, a Martin Luther dwarf, and many more.

According to some sources, there are over 700 little bronze statues in Wrocław. At some point, someone really should find out the actual number…

In any case, enthusiasm for the dwarfs among the people of Wrocław hasn't dissipated. In 2020, Tadeusz Gawęcki, the founder of Bar Witek – a snack bar known for its huge portions – died. Within days of his passing, a crowdfunding campaign was launched to have a dwarf dedicated to him. The 5000 zloty needed for this came together within a few days.

Every autumn, usually in September, the International Dwarf Festival takes place in Wrocław, with a large parade, a dwarf village, and many smaller events on the sidelines – the year's highlight for many families and visitors.

An overview map of the dwarfs is available online at www.krasnale.pl or at the tourist information office on the Market Square.

20 Film Location for Bridge of Spies
How satellite dishes turned into good financial investments

- Most scenes were shot around ul. Kurkowa and ul. Ptasia in Nadodrze, a few more at ul. Menniczna ◉ Plac Staszica ◉ All year round ◉ Most szpiegów ◉ almostginger.com/bridge-of-spies-film-locations-wroclaw
- The Narrow-gauge Railway Station is not far from here **48**

Steven Spielberg's *Bridge of Spies* is a 2014 spy thriller set in 1950s East Berlin about a lawyer, James Donovan (Tom Hanks), who negotiates the release of a pilot captured by the Soviet regime on behalf of the US government. How is Wrocław connected to a film set in East Berlin?

The set designer Adam Stockhausen, who even received an Oscar nomination for the film, had trouble finding a suitable film location in Germany. The atmosphere of the 1950s was to be captured, so the often-used film location Görlitz was ruled out as a production location for being too well renovated and not shabby enough. But when Stockhausen saw an old photo of Wrocław, he knew immediately that this was the right place. He scouted the location and was not disappointed! The decision to film in Wrocław – especially in the Nadodrze district – was made.

The filming itself was an extensive adventure. Checkpoint Charlie, for example, was recreated, and 90 metres of the Berlin Wall was erected on the temporary film set. A relatively large area was cut off for the filming, which caused a very mixed response from the local population. Some residents were upset about little things, such as the fact that they now had to walk two minutes longer to the bakery.

Others knew exactly how to take advantage of the situation. One of the hurdles of the production was that many houses had satellite dishes attached to them, a technology that did not exist in the 1950s. These dishes had to be removed for the filming. The residents affected by this received compensation and newly installed roof antennas. As the news of the compensation spread, satellite dishes suddenly appeared everywhere on the houses before filming began…

21 Four Domes Pavilion
Reanimated in the year of the Capital of Culture

F

- Wystawowa 1 🚋 Hala Stulecia 🕐 Tue–Thu 10–16h, Fri 12–20h, Sat–Sun 10–18h 🇵🇱 Pawilon Czterech Kopuł 🌐 mnwr.pl
- Free admission on Tuesdays (permanent exhibition only)
- Relax at Pergola and the Multimedia Fountain **68**

Built at the same time as the Centennial Hall and opened in 1913, the Four Domes Pavilion is another example of the innovative character from Wrocław's architectural scene. As the name promises, the monumental building from Hans Poelzig has exactly four symmetrically arranged domes. They are so ingeniously designed that the rectangular interior is filled with diffuse daylight via the incorporated skylights.

As with Max Berg's Centennial Hall, reinforced concrete technology was used here, a novelty at the time. Originally, the pavilion was intended purely as an exhibition space – as the first exhibition was opened to mark the 100th anniversary of the Battle of Leipzig.

After the Second World War, the Wrocław Film Factory used the building as a film studio. Unfortunately, this did not contribute to its maintenance, and frequent reconstruction work took the building further and further away from its original state.

Finally, in 2009, there was a change of ownership, and the city's National Museum could carry out extensive restoration between 2013 and 2015. The European Union largely absorbed the costs of around 84 million zloty.

In 2016, when Wrocław proudly held the title of the European Capital of Culture, the pavilion was reopened as a permanent host location for the Museum of Contemporary Art, a branch of the National Museum. Together with the Centennial Hall, it was recognised as a UNESCO World Heritage Site.

Today, numerous Polish works of art since the mid-20th century can be admired there. In particular, the sculptures by Magdalena Abakanowicz have proved to be a great magnet for visitors.

22 The Giant Concrete Chair

Out of place or exactly where it's supposed to be?

🚩 Rzeźnicza 12 🚇 Rynek 🕒 All year round ⭕ Krzesło Kantora
» Explore more art while enjoying a cappuccino at the Pomiędzy Café **71**

There are plenty of opinions about art, and taste is often subjective. The famous Polish writer, painter, and theatre director Tadeusz Kantor created a piece that confirms this with his giant concrete chair in Wrocław. As he has also dealt intensively with the subject of *chairs* in his theatre performances, the object as such is no surprise for him – but how did it come here?

As early as 1970, Kantor had sent the design for a colossal concrete chair to the artistic symposium in Wrocław. He said that the art did not come from the chair itself but from the environment. He suggested putting it somewhere close to traffic to impression of being deserted.

Although a commitment was made to install the chair as planned, it could also be interpreted as a mockery of the communist monuments of the time. This would be a big problem. Interestingly, the artist was aware of this, as he occasionally referred to his project as „the impossible sculpture."

It took 41 years until the idea was finally realised according to the original plans. When the sculpture was unveiled in 2011, Kantor's concerns about the old regime's sensitivities had become obsolete. Unfortunately, the artist could no longer attend in person, as he passed away in 1990.

(Interestingly, a similar wooden version was installed in Oslo in 1971. But it did not survive the Scandinavian weather conditions – another reason for choosing concrete as the material.)

The personal answer to the question „Is this art, or can we throw it away?" can be found between ul. Rzeźnicza and ul. Nowy Świat, where the eight-metre-high, eight-ton chair now stands directly on the busy ring road.

There is a higher probability that you might find people climbing it later at night, but we advise you to refrain from doing it yourselves due to the many stories about broken arms and legs.

23 Gondola Bay

A new perspective of the city – sunburn guaranteed

🗺 D

📍 Jana Ewangelisty Purkyniego 9   🚇 Urząd Wojewódzki
🕐 Daily 11–19h (April to October)   🔴 Zatoka Gondoli   🌐 zatokagondoli.pl
» Don't miss the rest of the Xawery Dunikowski Promenade, especially the National Museum **98**

How about an unusual view of Wrocław? After all, depending on how you look at it, the city is considered the Venice of the East or the Venice of the North, so there's no shortage of water. And, of course, we're not talking about hydroelectric power plants or beautiful water towers here, but about the opportunity to enjoy the city from a peaceful water perspective.

Not only is there more space out on the water than on the busy streets and squares, but more importantly: the magical views of the most beautiful places are guaranteed. Gondola Bay *(Zatoka Gondoli)* is undoubtedly one of the best starting points to experience the city from a new perspective. Boats and kayaks are available for hire – all powered by muscles. It's an excellent opportunity to eliminate some of the calories you've gained in Wrocław's cafés. But be careful, especially in the summer months, as the reflections of the water create a high risk of sunburn – be sure to bring a head covering and sunscreen.

Towards the city centre, kayaks and hand-steered boats are only allowed as far as Sand Island *(Wyspa Piasek)*. But that's quite enough to get a unique view of the panorama of Cathedral Island. In the other direction, it is worth stopping at ZaZoo or Odra Pany Beach Bar along the Oder River. These are beach bars with a small dock for kayaks and other boats.

A short detour into nature is also possible: just behind the Grunwaldzki Bridge, on the right, there is a small houseboat just behind Odra Centrum on the river banks. A small tributary of the Oder *(Oława)* flows out there. Once on it, a few curious ducks and other birds quickly surround you, while on the piers of a new residential area, you can observe the everyday life of Poles: fishing, flirting, and enjoying the summer in other ways.

24 Grunwaldzki Bridge

The longest suspension bridge in Poland – a prestige project

🚊 Most Grunwaldzki 🚌 Most Grunwaldzki 🕐 All year round
🚏 Most Grunwaldzki ⏩ Walk across the bridge towards the Manhattan Building Complex **36**

There was a desire to connect the two sides of the Oder River near the old town as early as the late 1880s, but as it happens often with larger construction projects, it takes time for ideas to be realised. It wasn't until several years later that all the necessary plots of land were purchased so that the design phase could begin.

In 1902, the city councillor for building, Richard Plüddemann, finally submitted the first draft and organised a competition in 1904, which architects Martin Mayer and Robert Weyrauch won. With the final concept, Wrocław demonstrated a high spirit of innovation and, as later with the Centennial Hall, performed a truly pioneering work of architecture.

With a length of 112.5 metres and a width of 18 metres, it is the longest suspension bridge in Poland – another superlative of the city. When built, it was a novelty that a special construction elastically absorbed the fluctuations. This was made possible with the steel strips running over rollers. It is also worth mentioning that this is a real suspension bridge without supporting pillars.

In 1910, after two years of construction, it was ceremoniously opened as the *Kaiserbrücke* – after Kaiser Wilhelm II. During the Weimar Republic, the bridge temporarily bore the name *Freiheitsbrücke* (Freedom Bridge, 1924-1933), but this was not accepted among the residents. So the bridge finally reverted to its first name. Today the bridge is called *Most Grundwaldzki* (Grunwaldzki Bridge) and is undoubtedly one of the most beautiful bridges on the Oder.

And what would an important building be without a suitable urban legend? Allegedly, a pilot in 1951 or 1952 flew underneath the bridge in a daring manoeuvre, with only great luck preventing a catastrophe. The suspected pilot, however, denied the accusations.

It is certainly interesting that there were other cheaper options on the table to connect the two banks of the Oder. Still, Plüddemann insisted on a variant that allowed a panoramic view of Cathedral Island.

25 The Heart of Nadodrze

The mosaic that unites an entire neighbourhood

📍 Paulińska 4/8 🚊 Paulińska 🕐 All year round ⊙ Mozaika Nadodrza
🌐 w-r.com.pl/projekty/mozaika-nadodrza » Either reward yourself with an ice cream from Lody Roma **33** or get a delicious cake from Pomiędzy Café **71**

Today's alternative district of Nadodrze used to have a somewhat dubious reputation and, until a few years ago, was one of the areas people preferred to avoid. The numerous parks were problem areas and hotspots of the local drug and alcohol scene. Since its transformation into an alternative quarter of Wrocław, which is very popular among hipsters, Nadodrze is often lovingly compared to Berlin-Kreuzberg. The diversity of people, stories, and fates hidden behind the old tenement facades from pre-war times is particularly characteristic of the neighborhood.

A fantastic idea to express this diversity is the so-called „Heart of Nadodrze." This is a project by local artists to bring new life and colour to this once less-relaxed area. The heart is a vibrant mosaic consisting of 433 tiles. However, they were not designed by those who started this initiative but by the neighborhood's residents. Local shops, kindergartens, institutions of all kinds, artisans, schools, pensioners, in fact, the entire spectrum of residents living here helped out. A different person individually decorated each tile, and together they make a beautiful mosaic heart.

This piece of art is easy to miss for unsuspecting bypassers, as it is located in a backyard at ul. Paulińska 4/8. This is extraordinary proof that the big picture is always the sum of many small parts – in this case, highly motivated people.

And it doesn't stop there. Many other projects have been kicked off since then. For example, there's the annual *Kinomural* event which takes place in the neighbourhood around the end of September. For this, the building facades are enlighted with audiovisual projections that were made by artists from all over the world. It is so popular amongst the citizens of Wrocław that it is not uncommon for the traffic to be a standstill in Nadodrze.

26 The Hidden Backyard of Gniazdo

A place to go not only for digital nomads

 C

- Świdnicka 36 Opera Daily 8–20h Gniazdo
- facebook.com/kawagniazdo Check out what happened to the plot of land where the famous postmodernist building Solpol used to be **72**

What do content creators, programmers, students, and authors in Wrocław have in common? They all populate Gniazdo, a popular place on the scene, not only because of the fast wifi access but also because of the selection of delicious coffees and the nicely designed modern surroundings. Gniazdo has another big plus that is not immediately obvious but has to be discovered first – we are talking about the hidden inner courtyard.

When you enter the café, you are first drawn to the colour-filled cake counter, the small souvenir shop with artistically inspired postcards and pins, or the other guests whose conversations enliven the café. It's all too easy to overlook the inconspicuous door at the back that leads to the inner courtyard.

The beautifully renovated courtyard is entirely enclosed by the walls of the building and is an ideal place to meet friends in peace or pursue other productive activities. Even the birds feel at home here and add to the atmosphere with their chirping. Add a little clattering from cups gently placed on saucers, and the soundscape is perfect. You can also enjoy everything from the cosy beach chairs in the courtyard.

Finally – the house coffee specialties. Those who like to experiment will undoubtedly find what they are looking for at Gniazdo with the Chilli Cappuccino or Tonic Espresso, available seasonally. The in-house baristas know their business and will find the right bean for every guest. The breakfast menu is extensive and offers something for every taste. Their signature dish *(Serniczki)* is a hint to the Ukrainian ownership and something you will hardly find in any other café in Wrocław. If you never had these delicious hot mini cheesecakes with the best quality cottage cheese, accompanied with three different fruity sauces to dip them in, you certainly have to try them out. And after breakfast, stay for their great bagels as well!

27 The Historic Market Square
One of the largest market squares in Europe

🚇 Rynek 1 🚊 Rynek 🕐 All year round 🇵🇱 Rynek
» Have a bargain meal at the Milk Bar Miś **39**

Wrocław's historic market square has been the city's heart for centuries. First delineated in the early 13th century, shortly after the Mongol invasion, the square is one of the largest in Europe. Its dimensions of 205 by 175 metres only rank slightly behind the record holders Kraków and Olecko.

Another highlight here is one of the oldest restaurants in Europe. Most sources date the opening of *Piwnica Świdnicka* to 1273, and countless litres of beer have been served and traditional dishes cooked in the cellar under the town hall since. Goethe and Chopin were guests here too.

The town hall itself is a masterpiece of Gothic architecture and one of the most impressive buildings in the city. Construction began in the 13th century but was not completed until the mid-16th century, as new elements were constantly added. The east side of the building, with the astronomical clock, is one of the most popular picture spots in the city.

Around the square are numerous restaurants, cafés, and clubs. Naturally, the prices here are somewhat higher than in the side streets of the city centre. And don't overlook the cute little alleys that run through the middle of the market square and the town hall.

The entire market square is surrounded by colourful houses in the Renaissance and Art Nouveau styles. However, most of them do not show off the original facades as a result of reconstruction – a large number of the buildings were destroyed during the Siege of Wrocław and rebuilt after the war. This reconstruction was an essential part of the efforts at the time to inspire more Poles to move to Poland's new western territories, especially with the help of optimistic-looking photographs.

Entire books have been written about the countless details on the houses around the market square. A popular game is to find the „fake window." One of the buildings has a window that is just a mural but hardly stands out.

As part of the post-war work, the statue of King Frederick William III was also removed from the market square and replaced in 1956 with a representation of Aleksander Fredro, a famous writer. The symbolism behind this is important, as that statue had previously stood in Lviv, a city that Poland had to cede to the Soviet Union. Thus, the expelled Poles from the former Eastern territories received a small point of reference.

A word to the wise: in the late hours, individual travellers and groups of men are often approached by young, friendly ladies and invited to clubs for drinks. It is better not to accept these invitations – too many visitors have woken up the following day with headaches on the edge of the Oder River after visiting very sketchy clubs with their credit cards maxed out...

28 The History Trail

*Crash course in history:
Wrocław in five minutes*

🔵 Plac Nankiera 15 🚋 Hala Targowa 🕐 All year round
⚪ Ścieżka historii Wrocławia ⏩ Visit the Market Hall **38**

Throughout its more than thousand-year history, numerous tragedies have occurred in Wrocław. Many may think primarily of the expulsions after the Second World War, which left many deep scars on both the Polish and German sides. But it is often overlooked that the city founded under the name Vratislavia has experienced many other rulership changes, so reducing it to the events of the last hundred years doesn't do justice to its history.

Of course, there is a significant amount of specialist literature on the turbulent history of Wrocław, but only a few read it in depth. So that no one has to return home wholly uneducated, the „History Trail" was created – presenting the most critical events in the history of Wrocław. And it quickly becomes clear why it is a small „Walk of Fame." Like the Hollywood stars, the most historical events are immortalised on the ground.

Around 1000 years of history can be easily „walked" through in less than five minutes. Those who have completed this walk may not be able to keep up with the readers of historical literature, but they will have gained a good overview of the main events in the city's history.

- **1000:** The Bishopric in Wrocław is established
- **1241:** The Mongol invasion
- **1242:** Municipal rights
- **1335:** Kingdom of Bohemia
- **1526:** Habsburg Monarchy
- **1530:** The current city coat of arms is established
- **1633:** Bubonic plague
- **1702:** The University is established
- **1741:** Silesia falls to Prussia
- **1793:** The Tailors' Revolution
- **1807:** The capitulation to Napoleon
- **1842:** The first railway line
- **1913:** The Centennial Hall opens
- **1945:** The Siege of Wrocław
- **1980:** The Solidarity Movement
- **1997:** The World Eucharistic Congress and the Millennium Flood
- **2012:** EURO 2012
- **2016:** The European Capital of Culture
- **2017:** The World Games

29 Kalambur

D

The meeting place of the artistic community

Kuźnicza 29A Uniwersytecka Sun–Wed 12–2h, Thu–Sat 12–4h
Art Cafe Kalambur kalambur.org Dress up the naked swordsman 47

As an integral part of the artistic scene, Kalambur has been well-covered in travel guides about Wrocław. And rightfully so!

Located at ul. Kuźnicza 29a since 1964, Kalambur has become an indispensable meeting place for culture, socialising, and nightlife. It was founded in 1957 by physics graduate Bogusław Litwiniec as the Kalambur Theatre. In 1983, the Kalambur Café finally opened as the pub that today's Wrocław residents know and love. But Kalambur has remained true to its roots: Not only does it have theatre, but also art exhibitions, concerts, readings, and other cultural events of all kinds.

Even before you enter, you are greeted artistically – by a life-size crocodile. But don't worry, it won't bite: its mouth is tied shut with the string of a balloon that pulls the crocodile towards the sky. The sculpture was created by Michał Staszczak in 2014 who was then an assistant professor at the Department of Sculpture of the Academy of Fine Arts in Wrocław. Not coming as a surprise, it represents the surreal experience and the different version of our reality you might find inside. Upon entering, it also quickly becomes clear that this is one of the most popular meeting places for musicians, writers, actors, and artists from all genres. And you will likely meet national celebrities there...

But the regular crowd consists of many students who come to work on their stuff in the afternoon and then stay for the evening programme. In a small corner kiosk window at the edge of the building, probably a former ticket booth, you'll get to the so-called *Kalapizza*. As the name suggests, this is the in-house pizzeria. Occasionally there are particular items on the menu, along with a free shot with every slice of pizza.

Cheers! Or even better in Polish - *Na zdrowie!*

30 Kolejkowo
A

Wrocław downsized – with great attention to detail

- Powstańców Śląskich 95 Wielka Daily 10–18h Kolejkowo
- wroclaw.kolejkowo.pl You'll find more railway and train history in the Neighborhood of Brochów 51

At first glance, Kolejkowo looks like a museum that revolves around a huge model railway. And indeed, this was undoubtedly the original idea. But in the meantime, the very special city life of Wrocław developed in the small, downsized world.

More than 14 kilometres of cable and almost a kilometre of tracks have been laid down to move the 27 trains with a total of 118 carriages. But the trains aren't the only moving parts here. Cars and other vehicles are also constantly moving through a magnetic system. Each train covers almost 400 kilometres per month, a great distance considering the average speed of just 1.5 km/h.

But even more fascinating than the model railway is the everyday life around it, as thousands of lovingly designed details can be found. In addition to a replica of the market square, you will be able to discover many other recognizable places, such as Hotel Monopol, the Solpol building (RIP), or even the Świebodzki railway station itself, where the Kolejkowo used to be located. The reconstruction of that station alone is said to have taken 2062 hours.

Most impressive are the depictions of the inhabitants. Numerous scenes make you smile: a wedding with obstacles, pigs escaping from cars, drunken construction workers, a dog that snatches a vital piece of clothing from a woman sunbathing, declarations of love on a bridge, and countless other everyday situations.

Even the time of day is programmed: The day lasts nine minutes, and in the four-minute-long night, new surprises appear in the illuminated windows of the apartment buildings. Some visitors may find it a bit overstimulating, but explorers will love Kolejkowo – making it an excellent destination for children and adults alike.

31 Kwiaty Kawy

A place of well-being for all your senses

- Plac Kościuszki 12 Arcady (Capitol)
- Daily 9–20h Kwiaty Kawy facebook.com/KwiatyKawyiInne
- Try to get access to some beautiful old staircases 4

Kwiaty Kawy started as a little flower shop at ul. Szczytnicka 44. Later, a few little tables were added. This allowed visitors to sit in a little jungle of plants and admire all the beautiful flower pots and other decorative elements – like golden framed mirrors or Venetian masks – while enjoying a delicious cup of coffee.

As residents quickly established Kwiaty Kawy as their favourite place, it was obvious that the three tables would not be able to cope with the demand. A second location was the next logical step. This one, at Plac Kościuszki 12, is more spacious and offers another 360-degree source of well-being in Wrocław. Kwiaty Kawy is particularly great for people who love the coziness of being surrounded by plants, but simply don't have the skills to keep plants alive in their own home – this author included.

Outside of the above-mentioned decorative elements, you will find a selection of books among the antique wooden tables and chairs – a mixture of vintage, modern, and even farmhouse styles – that create a place you will simply love to spend time in. And what's also refreshing is the non-traditional flower styles, like nothing you'd find at the Salt Market Square, but more modern-design-oriented. And they cover all the senses!

When you enter Kwiaty Kawy, close your eyes and take a deep breath. Although no scientific medical claims can be made at this point, the air inside is going to be much better than the thick blanket of smog covering Wrocław in the winter months. Your life might even be extended by a few days after a visit, who knows?

A Sunday brunch option has recently been added, so even more senses are being addressed. The brunch is vegetarian and a pleasure for the eyes and palate alike. Fresh fruits, different sorts of salads, hummus, bread, and much more are offered to get your Sunday started in the best possible way. Get all your senses involved here, and you'll find out why Kwiaty Kawy is truly an extraordinary place to be.

32 Leśnica Castle

Once burnt down by the residents of Wrocław

📍 Plac Świętojański 1 🚊 Leśnica 🕐 Mon–Fri 10–20h, Sat–Sun 10–18h
⛔ C.K. Zamek w Leśnicy 🌐 zamek.wroclaw.pl ≫ Since you are already exploring castles, go to Palace Pawłowice, which is a bit further out, but totally worth it 64

Leśnica Castle, like many of the city's buildings, can look back on a long, sometimes dramatic and exciting, history. In the early 12th century, probably in 1132, it was built as a princely seat for the ruling Piast dynasty.

As time passed, the owners changed regularly. They included Bohemian kings, various patrician families like one of the Silesian chamber presidents, crusaders of the Red Star, and many other characters from the wealthy upper class. Naturally, each owner wanted to remodel the castle according to their ideas, and so significant structural changes were made several times.

The castle was not immune to fire either; it last burned down in 1953 after surviving the war unscathed. However, the first fire engulfed the castle as early as 1459, when the inhabitants of Wrocław burned it down themselves – they feared that it might be taken by the then-Hussite king, and preferred to sacrifice it to the flames!

Today, the castle is used as a cultural centre, which is why numerous events and exhibitions take place there, as well as medieval markets and fantasy festivals. The Festival of Good Beer was also first held there before moving to the Stadium due to large demand.

Since the castle is only mentioned in a few travel guides, there are hardly any tourists there, although it can be reached easily by train, tram, or bicycle. This is the right place for castle lovers who prefer a photo without crowds. And the surrounding park invites you to take a short walk and offers a relaxing contrast to the hustle and bustle of the city – also ideally suited for catching your breath before the return journey.

33 Lody Roma Ice Café

The first ice cream after the war – and still one of the best in town!

📍 Ludwika Rydygiera 5 🚋 Dubois 🕐 In summer 11–19:30h
🇵🇱 Lodziarnia Roma 🌐 lodyroma.pl » Take your ice cream and walk towards the colourful backyards of Nadodrze to explore some street art **17**

On sunny days, there is often a long queue of people in front of the huge Nadodrze graffiti leading toward the district's entrance. Their destination is not recognisable at first glance until you see the stream of happy people strolling in the opposite direction with ice cream in their hands. That's right; the often impressive queue is full of ice cream-hungry people who can't wait to get a scoop of their favourite ice cream at Lody Roma!

The oldest ice cream parlour in Wrocław opened in 1946, the year after the war ended. Just after electricity and water were reconnected in the building, Antoni Grzelak, an Italian pastry chef and pilot, opened the Lody Roma ice cream parlour. Since then, the best ice creams in Wrocław have been made there using natural ingredients and traditional Italian recipes. When Grzelak moved to Warsaw in 1962, his brother took over the ice cream parlour, which he ran for decades until he finally passed it over to Jerzy Góralski in 1991.

At Lody Roma, time seems to have stood still. Not much has changed since 1946, neither the location nor the traditions and recipes. Even payment is the same as ever: with plastic chips sold at the cash register. But nowadays, as is the case almost everywhere in Poland, credit cards are also accepted.

Over the years, many unusual ice creams have been added to the classics. The ice cream parlour is known nationwide for its black sesame, beetroot, and pumpkin flavours. And „national" doesn't just mean Poland – Lody Roma made it onto the Guardian's "20 of Europe's best ice-cream parlours" list in 2018.

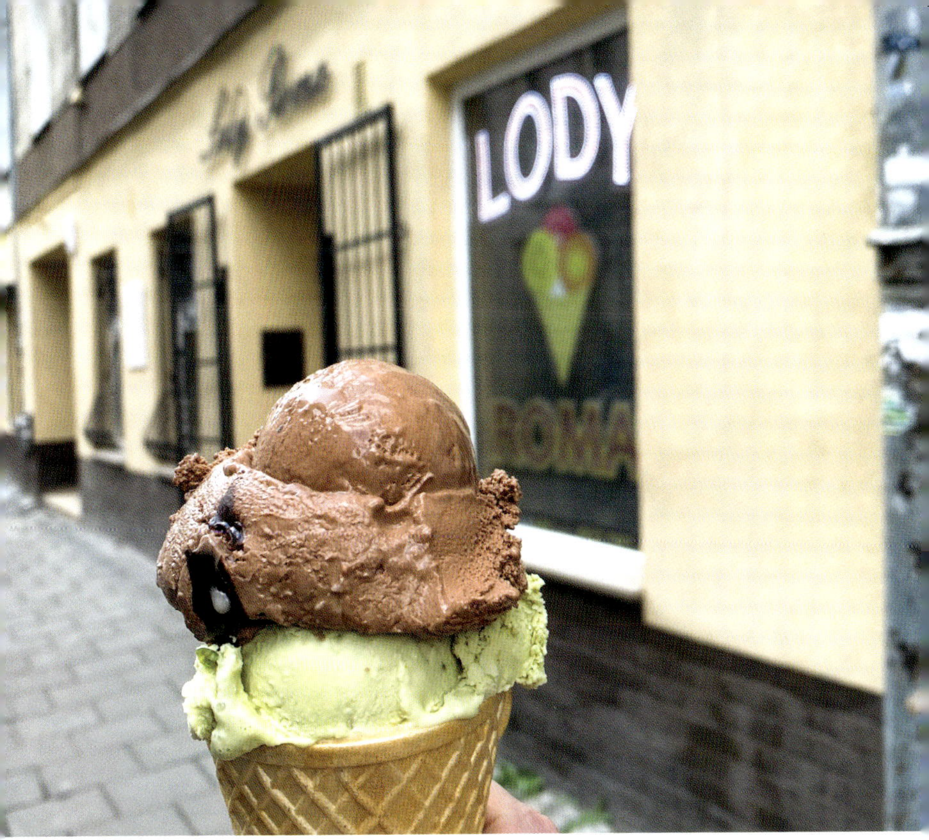
Lody Roma
LODY
ROMA

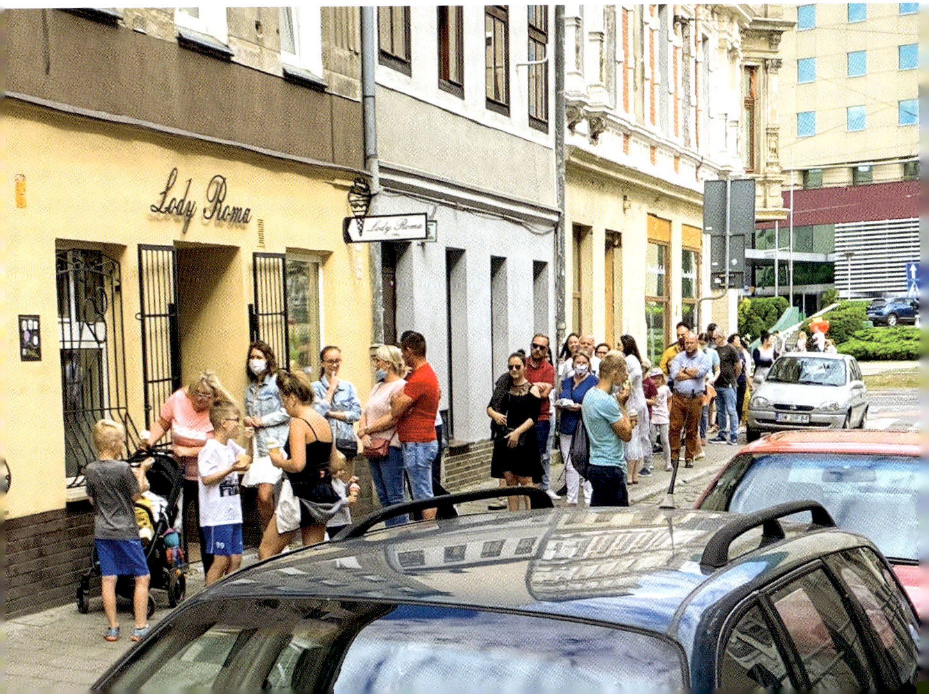
Lody Roma
Lody Roma

34 Macondo

Where stamp workshops meet Japanese calligraphy classes

Pomorska 19 Pomorska Daily 12–20h Macondo
macondofundacja.weebly.com Visit the Heart of Nadodrze 25

It's hard to explain what Macondo is in just a few words. Some might say it's a small, playful café full of bric-a-brac. Others consider it first and foremost a cultural and meeting point. But there are certainly people who see it as a place for further individual education – or as a bookshop, concert venue, small art-house cinema, source of inspiration, and much more.

The name Macondo is based on the place of the same name in what is probably the most famous work by the Colombian Nobel Prize winner for literature, Gabriel García Márquez, *One Hundred Years of Solitude*. There are certainly few places where Japanese calligraphy courses are as much a matter of interest as workshops on stamp making or violin concerts.

The sustainability aspect is crucial at Macondo, underlined by a regular clothing exchange. But it's not only clothes that are exchanged here. How about the plant exchange, where overwhelmed plant owners can pass on their plants to more knowledgeable owners? The book and record exchange is so regular that it almost doesn't need to be mentioned. How about a theatre workshop? Or a ceramics workshop? Meetings with writers? Poetry slams? Discussions on how the brain works, led by molecular biologists? Why not learn how to draw, make your own notebooks, or conjure up a chocolate fondue?

Ultimately, it doesn't matter what you call Macondo because boredom will certainly not be a problem there. Many of the events are offered free or for a small donation. An insider piece of advice is the book box, where you can always find real bargains! And, of course, you will often come across the name Gabriel García Márquez there...

35 Mała Czarna

A well-hidden local coffee roastery

B

- Aleja Ignacego Jana Paderewskiego 35
- Stadion Olimpijski
- Mon–Fri 8–20h, Sat–Sun 10–20h
- Mała Czarna–Kawiarnia
- malaczarnacoffee.com
- Walk through Szczytnicki Park 85

Anyone heading for the Mała Czarna coffee roastery might be irritated to see a large sign with the words „CAMPING." Only at a second glance does it become clear that the offensively advertised campsite cannot be the reason for the gathering of people near the oversized banner. This is the location of one of the most popular local coffee roasteries, whose name means something like „little black one."

Its location is quite surprising – most wouldn't stray there by accident. But the regular visitors are always happy to make the long journey to enjoy the coffee specialties brewed there. The world's second most traded raw material – yes, coffee beans – is processed there with great attention to detail. For example, the packaging bears the colours of the Flavour Wheel widely used in the barista scene.

The café is located in a small brick bungalow that looks like the reception office of a campsite from the outside. The surprise is all the greater when you discover the roastery next door inside a modern sea container, inspired by the Tiny House movement. In summer, deckchairs and euro pallets in the garden invite you to spend a cosy afternoon with coffee and cake.

If you still have time afterward, you can explore some sights nearby. A visit to Mała Czarna can easily be combined with a tour of the Olympic Stadium and the Centennial Hall or a stroll in Szczytnicki Park. Thanks to the proximity of the Oder River, a bicycle tour is also a good idea. And another hidden gem for architecture fans: a house built as an igloo can be found around the corner at ul. Stanisława Moniuszki 33.

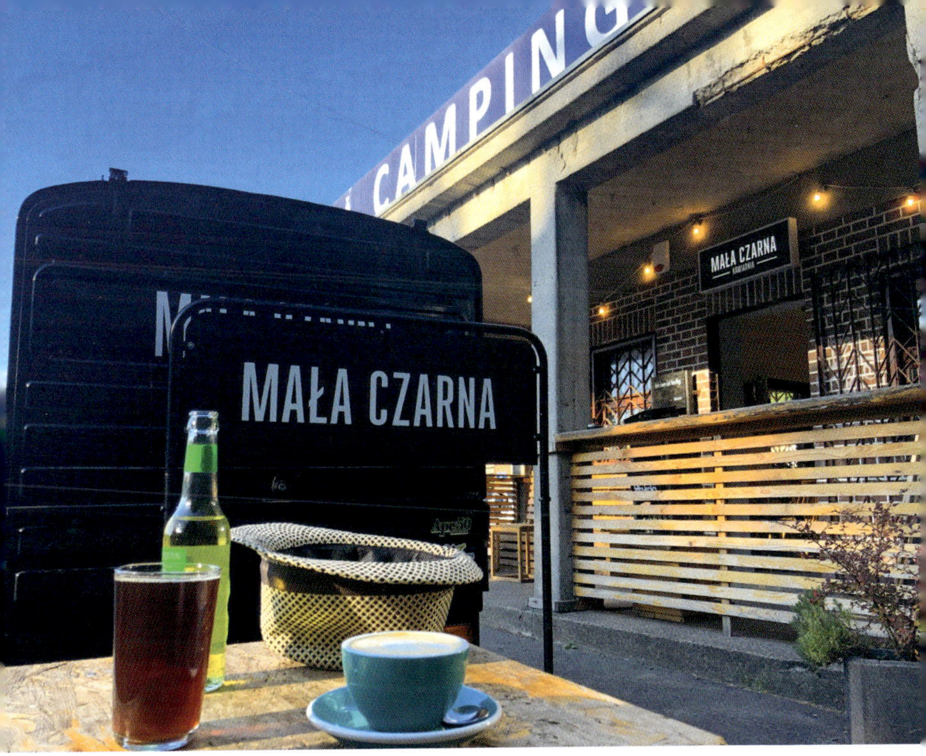
CAMPING
MAŁA CZARNA
MAŁA CZARNA

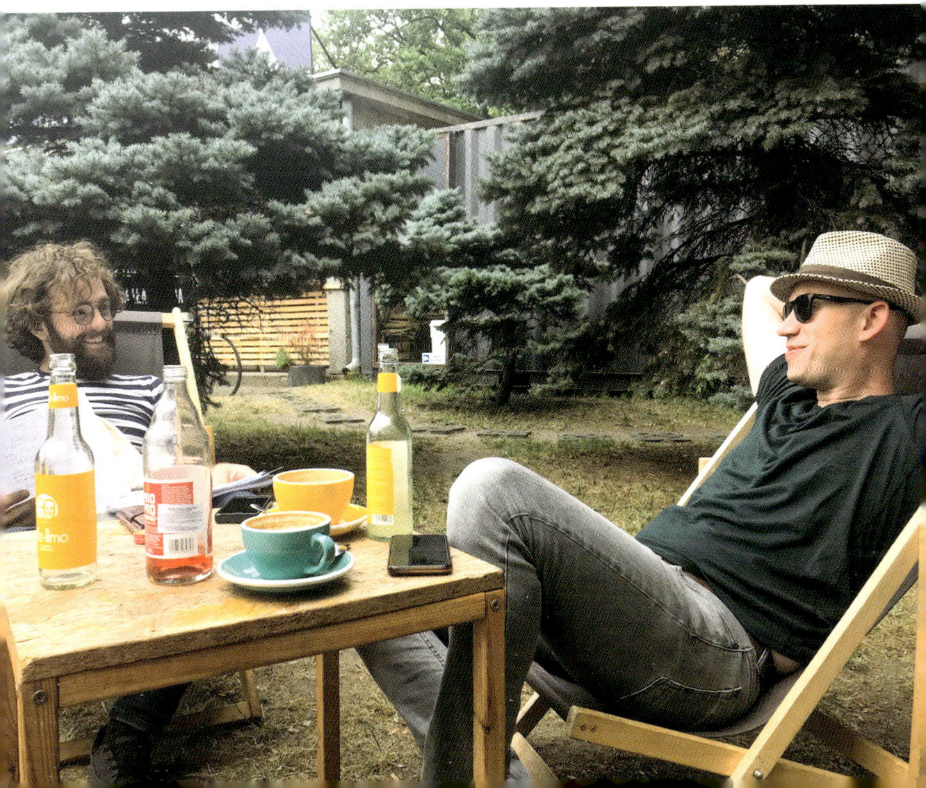

36 Manhattan Building Complex

The city's most popular black-and-white picture spot

F

- Plac Grunwaldzki 4
- Most Grunwaldzki
- All year round
- Manhattan („Sedesowce")
- Cross the river and enjoy the beautiful views from Odra Centrum **57**

Anyone crossing the Grunwaldzki Bridge from the city centre finds themselves on the other side of the Oder River and a somewhat different world. This world is dominated by six 55-metre-high residential complexes built in 1973 in the avant-garde style according to a design by Jadwiga Grabowska-Hawrylak.

Initially, plants were supposed to climb up the concrete facade, and a green roof terrace was planned. Still, the lack of money during the construction phase prevented the implementation of these features. The buildings, which might also be attributed to Brutalism, have blended into the skyline of Wrocław and are now listed monuments.

Their official name – Grunwaldzki Real Estate Square Complex – sounds too cumbersome, which is why the name „Manhattan" – in reference to New York – has become popular among the residents. The name „toilet blocks" is also often used.

In contrast to many other high-rise buildings, these hardly house any office or commercial spaces, just traditional living spaces. The view over the city from the upper floors is undoubtedly breathtaking. Thanks to its proximity to the Grunwaldzki campus, a collection of many university-related institutes, Manhattan has developed into a small student district. As a result, many new meeting places with an alternative touch have sprung up. One of them is *w kontakcie*, a vegan/vegetarian breakfast café that specialises in hummus and enjoys enormous popularity.

Until recently, there was a vintage market and food trucks at the bottom of the buildings. Unfortunately, demolition and revitalisation work in 2021 drove these creative spirits back to other parts of the city. But the Remont Bar, an absolute student classic in the neighbourhood, continues to hold its roots and is a great replacement, at least until the craft beer truck returns.

37 The Marina Topacz Sports Harbour

It doesn't have to be Saint-Tropez all the time!

🚌 Księcia Witolda 2　🚇 Uniwersytet Wrocławski　🕒 All year round
🇵🇱 Marina Topacz　» Test the acoustic mirrors on the Boulevard of Physicists **1**

The Marina Topacz sports harbour is a little piece of luxury right on the edge of the historic city centre. It quickly brings memories of the marinas of wealthy coastal cities – after all, this is probably the most expensive mooring opportunity for motor boats in the entire region. Many of them are privately owned and are very popular for small family trips on the Oder River. And not just motor boats, but also floating donuts and modern solar-powered boats are rented out to locals and visitors alike.

The whole area is framed by impressive modern residential and commercial estates, which were built between 2006 and 2012. The roof terraces, which promise a fantastic view, can certainly make you envious. Especially in the evening hours, a romantic atmosphere prevails there, when the reflections of the water are at their best, and the university, which takes up most of the sightseeing area towards the south, is touched by the warm sunlight.

This atmosphere is best enjoyed in one of the upscale restaurants located in the sports harbour. For example, Restauracja Przystań & Marina offers not only the panorama described above but also great international cuisine, and OK Wine Bar offers a huge selection of wines and exquisite fish dishes – both places are ideal for business and private occasions.

Incidentally, right next to the harbour is the historic hydroelectric power station based on the designs by Max Berg, the architect of the Centennial Hall. Built in 1921-1924, the station is miles away from the Centennial Hall in terms of architectural complexity but is convincing with its simplicity.

38 Market Hall

Once upon a time, human flesh was on offer

D

- Piaskowa 17
- Hala Targowa
- Mon – Sat 8 – 18:30h
- Hala Targowa
- visitwroclaw.eu/miejsce/hala-targowa
- Move on to Sand Bridge and Cathedral Bridge **79**

The market hall may initially appear to be a conventional tourist attraction, but behind its walls are fates and stories. Originally, there were plans for a total of four market halls in Wrocław, but only two of them were realised. The second hall, located on today's ul. Kolejowa was heavily destroyed during the war. Its ruins remained until 1973 when the final decision was made not to rebuild it.

Today's market hall *(Hala Targowa)* was first opened in 1908 and survived the war. After temporary use as a horse stable, the hall soon regained its original purpose. From 1980 to 1983, it was extensively restored, and in 2016 the facade underwent another rejuvenation.

Around 200 stalls on two levels welcome hungry visitors and tourists today. In addition to the typical market products such as fruit, vegetables, bakery goods, and meat products, you'll come across a few unusual offerings. For example, a coffee roastery, a small print shop, a craft beer bar, and a tea room with an almost endless assortment. Part of Wrocław's culinary scene also stocks up on fresh goods there.

On Saturdays, the market hall is transformed into a vast social potpourri of the most diverse groups: tourists meet Wrocław residents, and less fortunate residents sit with business people in a milk bar – a place for cheap food – in the entrance area. The daily life of Wrocław is fluidly mixed there with a touch of the holiday atmosphere.

At the back of the hall, Filip Kucharczyk runs Café Targowa – an 8 square metre café with only a few seats. Many advised him against this location initially, but he had the right instinct and created one of the most popular places to go for a short coffee break. In 2016, he also won the title of AeroPress World Champion – this accomplishment is even more impressive as he had nearly forgotten about the competition on his calendar.

But times were not always so harmonious. In 1924, a gentleman named Karl Denke was arrested not far away from Breslau. He was alleged to have sold human flesh labelled as pork in the market hall over some time. When his house was searched after his arrest, human remains were found next to the meat grinder, which could be identified as 40 different people – he had kept meticulous records. In his hometown, now Ziębice, a museum of household goods has even dedicated a small exhibition to Denke's horrific deeds.

39 Milk Bar Miś

The cult of cheap self-service restaurants

Kuźnicza 48 Uniwersytet Wrocławski Mon–Fri 8–18h, Sat 8–17h
Bar mleczny Miś Admire the beautiful University of Wrocław 92

If you haven't visited a milk bar at least once, you haven't really been to Poland – you often hear this sentence one way or another. It's hard to disagree because the self-service canteens from socialist times are places where time seems to have stood still. Towards the end of the 19th century, the first milk bar opened in Warsaw, and many more sprouted up like mushrooms after the First World War. But why are these cheap self-service restaurants called milk bars?

In the beginning, they mainly served vegetarian dishes based on milk, eggs, and flour. Today they often have a huge selection, including meat-based options, which started at the beginning of the 1990s. By far, the most popular milk bar in Wrocław is Miś at ul. Kuźnicza 48, where long queues of hungry people often wait to fill their bellies with good homemade Polish food at bargain prices. The prices are unbeatable: a complete meal can be purchased for three euros, and a bowl of soup costs less than one euro.

The colourful mix of guests also adds a great touch. Those who initially believe that this particular type of restaurant mainly attracts a poor clientele are surprised to discover that the entire spectrum of society meets for *obiad* (lunch). Children and seniors, rich and poor, students and workers, sweatpants and suits – many other contrasts can be observed there.

Of the more than 40,000 state-run milk bars in Poland, only about 140 have survived. They are now all in private hands and receive only minimal government support. The best locations in the city centres are highly sought after, and gentrification is doing the rest.

If you want to avoid the queue in front of the most famous milk bar in Wrocław but still don't want to miss out on the special milk bar flair, we recommend the nearby Bar Witek. You can get lavishly filled toast and *zapiekanka* – the Polish hybrid dish of pizza and baguette – served with similar vibes.

ZUPY MLECZNE
Mleczna z makaronem
Mleczna z kaszą manną
Mleczna z kaszą gryczaną
DANIA ŚNIADANIOWE
Bułka
Masło
Ser topiony
Dżem
Miód
Ser żółty
Twarożek ze śmiet i szczypiorkiem
Jajecznica na margarynie
Jajecznica na maśle
Jajko sadzone
Jajko gotowane
Parówki z wody
Ketchup Musztarda Majonez
DESERY
Kompot
Galaretka owocowa
Budyń ze śmietaną i cukrem
Sok naturalny
Sok zagęszczany na porcje
NAPOJE MLECZNE
Inka z mlekiem
Kakao
Śmietana
Kwaśne mleko
Kefir
Mleko
ZUPY
Pomidorowa z makaronem
Pomidorowa z ryżem
Grochowa
Kalafiorowa (z ziemniakami)
Pieczarkowa z makaronem
Barszcz czerwony z fasolą
Barszcz czerwony z krokietem
Brokułowa (krem) z grzankami
MĄCZNE
Pier ruskie z tł i cebulką (garmażerka)
Naleśniki z serem śmietaną i cukrem
Leniwe z cukrem i bułką tartą
Racuchy z jabłkami
Kopytka z sosem grzybowym
Łazanki z kapustą
Ryż z jabłkami śmietaną i cukrem
Makaron 4 sery z brokułami
Kluski śląskie z sosem
Pierogi ze szpinakiem
Krokiety z serem i pieczarkami
SURÓWKI
Surówka z białej kapusty
Surówka z kiszonej kapusty
Sałatka z czerwonej kapusty
Surówka z kapusty pekińskiej
Surówka z marchewki
Sałatka z buraczków
Surówka z selera
Mizeria
Surówka z pomidorów
Sałatka szwedzka
Surówka Colesław
Surówka z pora
Kapusta zasmażana
Buraczki zasmażane
Szpinak
Marchewka z groszkiem
Sałatka wiosenna
Fasolka szparagowa z bułką tartą
Kalafior z bułką tartą
Sałatka kalafior, brokuły z majonez
Surówka z rzodkwi
Surówka z papryki
MIĘSNE
Kotlet schabowy
Kotlet mielony
Kotlet De volaille
Kotlet schabowo - drobiowy
Kotlet drobiowy
Gulasz wołowy
Pulpety w sosie borowikowym
DANIA JARSKIE
Sos grzybowy
Sos pomidorowy
Gołąbki z grzybami
Fasolka po bretońsku
POLMIĘSNE
Placki ziemniaczane
Gulasz do placków
Pierogi z mięsem
Pyzy z mięsem
Sos, tłuszcz - płatne dodatki
RYBNE
Filet z mintaja
DODATKI DO DRUGICH DAŃ
Ziemniaki z tłuszczem
Kasza pęczak z tł.
Kasza gryczana z tłuszczem
Kasza gryczana z sosem
Kasza jaglana z tł.
Kasza jęczmienna z tł.
Kasza jęczmienna z sosem grz.
Ryż z tłuszczem
Coca-Cola
Oranżada
Woda cyranka
Tymbark - napój
Tymbark - sok
Herbata z cukrem i cytryną
Kawa z cukrem i śmietanką
polecamy do posiłków
fuzetea
JAK JEST ZIMA TO MUSI BYĆ ZIMNO
PO ODEJŚCIU OD KASY REKLAMACJI GOTÓWKOWYCH NIE UWZGLĘDNIA SIĘ.
OSÓB POD WPŁYWEM ALKOHOLU NIE OBSŁUGUJEMY!!
INFORMUJEMY, PROWADZIMY SPRZEDAŻ NA WYNOS
Pojemniki na wynos płatne:
TORBA PAPIEROWA 1 SZT - 1,00 zł
SCENA KAMIENICA
STYCZEŃ 2022
LUTY 2022
MARZEC 2022
MILORD DE PARIS
GALA WIEDEŃSKA

40 Mleczarnia

A rustic venue for any time: day and night

- Pawła Włodkowica 5 Narodowe Forum Muzyki Daily 8–4h, Sun until 0h Mleczarnia mleczarnia.wroclaw.pl
- Kalambur might still be open 29

Cosiness has a name: Mleczarnia. Its reputation as one of the city's most popular meeting places is highly deserved because of its cosy, rustic atmosphere. The pub is the perfect all-rounder for all occasions – whether it's a birthday party, a work meeting, an intimate chat in the afternoon, an intense philosophical conversation over a glass of wine, a hangover breakfast, or just a happy get-together with friends. The quaint black-and-white photos on the walls, the colourful upholstered wooden chairs, the soft romantic candlelight atmosphere, the huge carpets on the dark wooden floor, and the slightly dusty lampshades – all these characteristics and more provide a great sense of homeliness.

It's a miracle that Mleczarnia has not yet introduced the 24-hour opening. In the morning, a delicious breakfast is served, and in the warmer months, the terrace under the large chestnut tree offers a few free rays of sunshine, garnished with a view of the White Stork Synagogue. At lunchtime, Mleczarnia transforms into a bistro with a French charm. On rainy autumn days, you risk being absorbed by the enticing interior. In the evening, birthday parties are held there, or you can meet up with work colleagues or friends. In the late hours, especially during the week, you can sometimes see a few Wrocław residents stumbling in, happy that Mleczarnia is still open – as the last resort of the night, so to speak until the doors are locked there as well.

If you want to spend a whole weekend there – and there are plenty of reasons to do so – you can book a room in the adjoining Mleczarnia hostel. By the way, concerts, readings, and smaller events, such as stand-up comedy shows (often in English), regularly take place in the basement. It's always worth taking a look at Mleczarnia's event calendar.

41 The Monument of Common Memory
Memories of the past inhabitants of Wrocław

🎯 Eugeniusza Romera 🚊 Grabiszyńska (Cmentarz II) 🕒 All year round
🔴 Pomnik Wspólnej Pamięci ›› Visit the Zajezdnia History Centre **99**

The history of Wrocław was dramatically influenced by decisions taken at the end of the Second World War. Immeasurable suffering was created not just from the insane decision made by the Nazis to declare Wrocław a fortress *(Festung Breslau)*, but also from the expulsion of millions of people from numerous nationalities.

When the decision was made at the Potsdam Conference to move Poland's territory westwards, it was said that the resulting resettlement would take place in accordance with humanitarian imperatives. However, three times as many people had to be resettled than initially estimated, obviously with significant implications.

Today it is clear that this was the largest ethnic expulsion in history. More than twelve million people were eventually forced to leave their homes, often overnight and with only the bare necessities. In the utopian imaginings of the victorious powers, it must have seemed easy to displace over 2.5 million people in just over two months. Of course, the railway capacities could not cope with that many families, and Germans, Poles, Ukrainians, and Belarusians had to move in long marches by foot to an unknown place they were supposed to call their new homes.

For many years, this was a delicate subject for the new Polish residents of Wrocław. A majority of them were expelled from former eastern Polish territories; hence, there was even a basic empathy for the individual fates of the people forced to leave Wrocław. There were even circumstances where Germans and Poles had to share their homes for a certain period before the departure, and it is hard to imagine how awkward some of those situations must have been.

In the aftermath of the war, most of the German cemeteries were destroyed as well. However, to commemorate all of these people, a monument in Grabiszynski Park was erected in 2008 to remember those who previously lived in Wrocław – no matter if they were German, Polish, Catholic, Protestant, Jewish, or other. The Monument of Common Memory honors all the cemeteries that no longer exist by displaying some of the preserved tombstones as part of a 60-metre long wall.

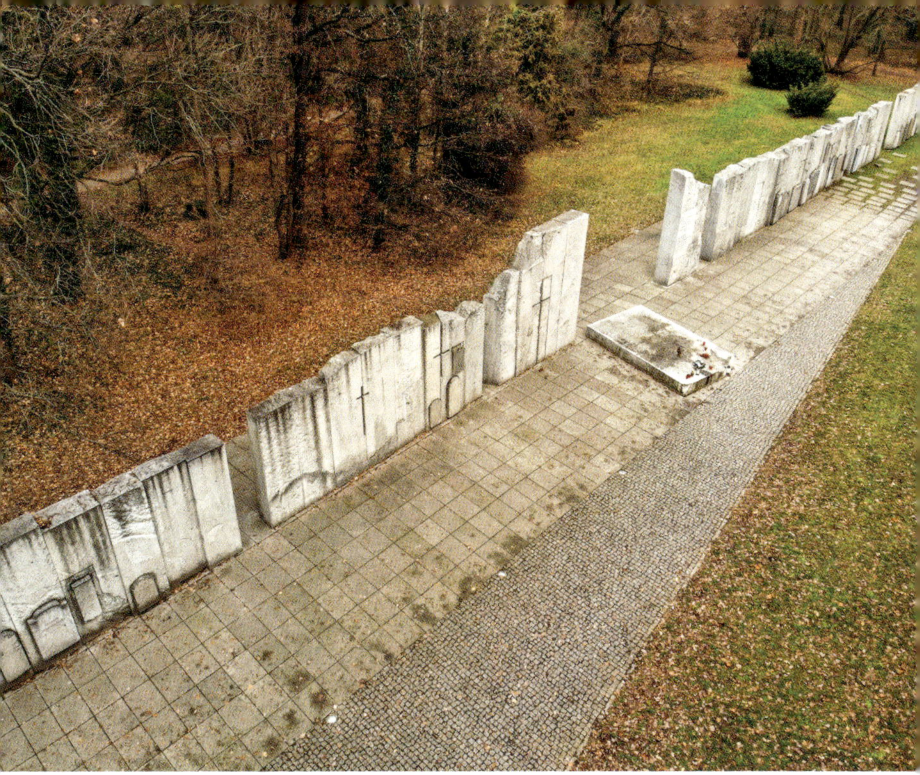

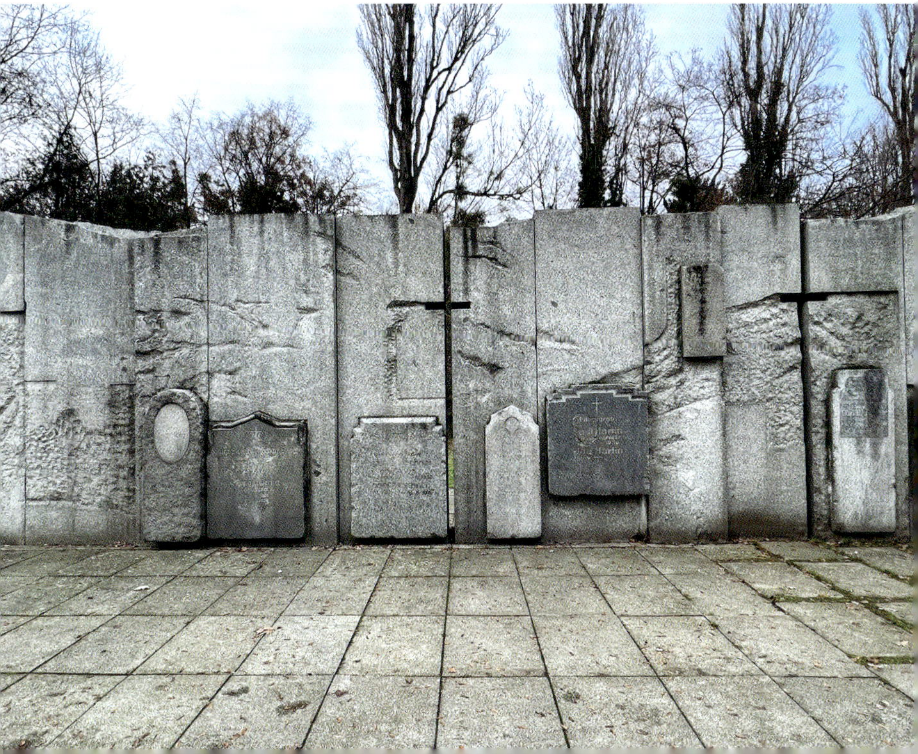

42 The Monument of the Anonymous Pedestrians

One of the most creative sculptures in the world

- Piłsudskiego 56 Arkady (Capitol) All year round
- Pomnik Anonimowego Przechodnia we Wrocławiu
- How about a coffee at Kwiaty Kawy? 31

The Polish word *przejście* (passage) is the original title of the Monument of the Anonymous Pedestrians. Its unique feature lies in its clairvoyant powers because the group of sculptures designed by Jerzy Kalina was exhibited before the events attributed to it today even occurred.

The monument consists of 14 bronze sculptures, each depicting life-size people. Seven descend into the underground on one side of the street, while the other seven ascend on the opposite side. The artwork was unveiled on the night of 12 December 2005, a carefully chosen date: exactly 24 years earlier, martial law had been declared to suppress the anti-communist movement. Martial law remained in force until July 1983. Quite a few people were murdered or disappeared under questionable circumstances during this period.

One of the most common interpretations of the installation is that the descent represents the declaration of martial law in 1981, which forced the opposition movement to go underground. The ascent on the other side of the street then symbolises the revival of Polish society after 1983. However, since this cannot be the original context – the original was exhibited in Warsaw in 1977, long before those events – which leaves, of course, some space for further interpretations.

This extraordinary monument is also well recognised in professional circles. In spring 2015, it was named one of the most creative sculptures in the world by the reputable magazine *Arch2O*. According to the US magazine *Newsweek*, the monument is one of the 15 most beautiful things to see in Poland. Incidentally, the original from 1977 is now also placed in Wrocław, in the Museum of Contemporary Art at the Four Domes Pavilion – a great indoor alternative in case it rains.

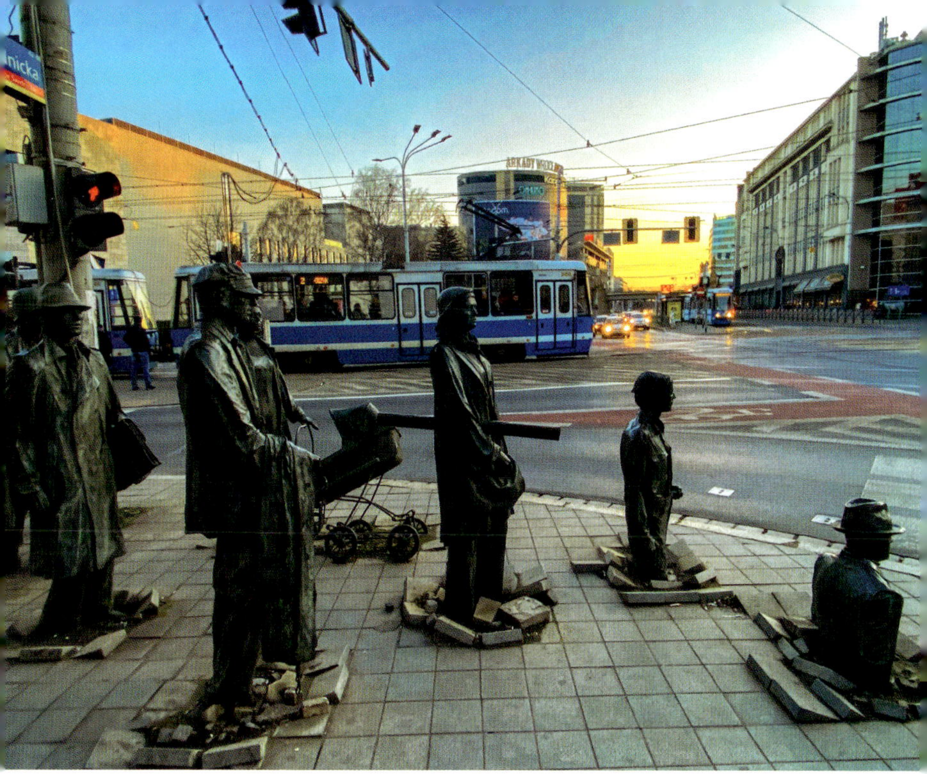

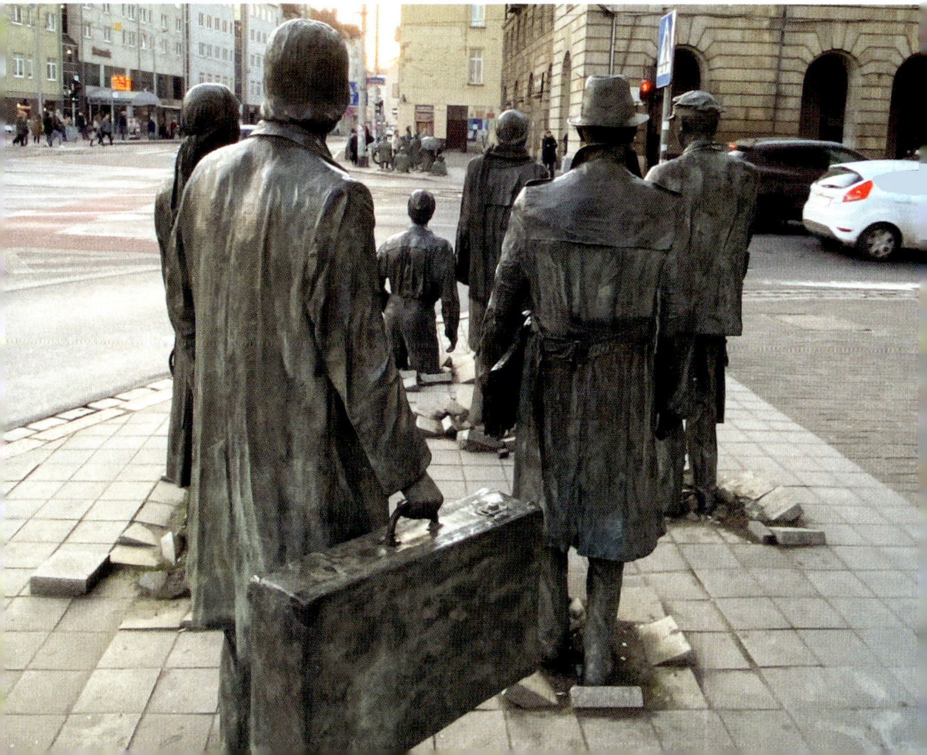

43 The Most Beautiful Street in Wrocław

A beauty that comes from its normality

◐ Norwida 🚋 Plac Grunwaldzki 🕐 All year round ⦵ Norwida
» Explore the Manhattan Building Complex **36**

The special charm of ul. Cypriana Kamila Norwida, often just called *ul. Norwida* is not immediately apparent. It is an ordinary street in a residential area, and no castles or monuments were discovered there, and no notable historical events took place there. Even the architecture is relatively usual for the period in which the street was built. To recognise something unusual, you have to look a little closer.

It is one of the few streets in Wrocław where the pre-war houses have been almost entirely preserved – and have now also been completely renovated. This was the result of an urban planning experiment in 2007. Until then, the city had almost exclusively renovated the buildings it owned. As part of the experiment, however, homeowner associations received a cost subsidy of 70% on the sole condition that an entry was made in the register of listed buildings. This concept was very successful and has already contributed to beautifying the entire townscape. The doorways, with their pretty decorations, are worth a look.

The entire street, previously *Hansastraße* during German times, not only gives the impression of what Wrocław once may have looked like but also allows a look into the future of the Nadodrze district, which is still home to a large number of pre-war houses in need of renovation.

Another notable feature are the trees on the street, a rarity in Wrocław residential areas. The tall trees on the west side provide a green living atmosphere. Residents looking out of their windows feel that they are living in the middle of a park.

Many students can be found, not because of its location right next to the Wrocław University of Technology campus, but more likely because the copy shop with the longest opening hours in the city is there. It is not uncommon to see students in a hurry shortly before midnight with panic-stricken faces.

44 The Museum of Games and Computers of the Past Era

From Pac-Man to the Commodore 64 to the Super Nintendo

Plac Orląt Lwowskich 20A Plac Orląt Lwowskich Tue–Sun 10–18h, Sat until 20h Muzeum Gry i Komputery Minionej Ery (Muzeum Gier) gikme.pl Try some street food and discover the old Świebodzki Railway Station 84

There is a place in Wrocław where time travel is no longer a fantasy of the future but a reality: The Museum of Games and Computers of the Past Era is undoubtedly the most important address in the city for computer game lovers. But it's not only nerds who find the place full of memories and nostalgia – everyone born in the 80s and 90s will easily relate to the exhibits.

However, the museum's start wasn't an easy one more than ten years ago. The necessary capital was raised through crowdfunding, and the search for a suitable location in the city took more than half a year. Finally, the museum was built in a former boxing club.

Of course, the exhibition is not just limited to computer games. Video game consoles from Nintendo, Sega, Sony, and other well-known manufacturers are also represented. For example, handhelds such as the Nintendo Game Boy and complete arcade machines such as racing simulators and pinball games are on display. The collection is growing steadily, and occasionally unannounced parcels arrive with new donations for the exhibition.

If you think this is just one of those exhibitions with dusty equipment and televisions behind a glass panel, you are mistaken: most of the museum is interactive! You can spend hours playing Pac-Man, Super Mario Kart, Doom, Street Fighter, Prince of Persia, Ping Pong, Space Invaders, and many other classics. When was the last time you had the chance to sit in front of an Atari or Commodore 64?

It is also interesting to look at the differences between western computer game culture and the communist-influenced east. This museum is a hidden gem for families with children, especially since it is rarely mentioned in traditional travel guides. The only problem is that time flies by, and it isn't open around the clock (yet).

45 The Mysterious Hand
No one knows where it came from

📍 E

● Strażnicza 1-3 🚇 Dubois 🕐 All year round 🔴 Instalacja artystyczna DŁOŃ
» Spend some time at Słodowa Island **81**

Wherever you live, you regularly walk past many places obliviously once you've established a routine. Suppose you cross University Bridge walking from Nadodrze towards the direction of the city centre. In that case, you will be delighted by the sight of the huge baroque facade of the university. Although the sculpture commemorating the Millennium Flood disaster of 1997 (as brought to life in the 2022 Netflix miniseries *High Water*) is visible on the bridge – a memorial to those who helped to rescue books – one tiny detail remains hidden from most people. There is a small mysterious hand in the walls of the bridge at the corner of ul. Strażnicza.

Apparently, someone was walled in there several years ago and is now desperately trying to escape – but, unfortunately, help came too late. This is a wonderful example of an everyday contemporary piece of art in Wrocław, and despite research, it is not clear who the artist was.

Perhaps it is one of the helping hands that rescued the books themselves during that flood disaster? Maybe someone forgot part of their Halloween costume, which has been stuck on the wall for years? Or is the connection between the hand and the wall meant to make us think? What is certain is that creative interpretations are required here until the artist is discovered and the matter is resolved.

The contemporary museum *(Muzeum Współczesne Wrocław)* inside a former air-raid shelter is also highly recommended for those who like this sort of art. The artists' names are guaranteed to be attributed to the art objects there.

💡 This is one of the sculptures to commemorate the "Millennium Flood".

46 Nafta Neo Bistro

A restaurant in a former secret place

B

🌐 Krakowska 180 🚊 Karwińska 🕐 Tue – Fri 17 – 23h, Sat 14 – 23h, Sun 14 – 21h   🍽 Nafta Neo Bistro
🌐 facebook.com/naftaneobistro, reservations under +48 450 050 180
» Mleczarnia might still be open **40**

Dinner at the Nafta Neo Bistro is undoubtedly one of the more unusual restaurant visits. Most people pick a restaurant based on a menu or after intensive research on websites and travel guides. In Wrocław, however, there is one restaurant that you can't stumble on by chance and doesn't stand out with great visibility. This is certainly also because the address was not publicly known until recently, reservations were only accepted by phone, and the directions were only sent by text message on the day of the reservation.

There is no doubt about it: Nafta is an extraordinary place where the chef pays great attention to the excellent quality of the ingredients, and sets the highest standards in service. The staff know all the dishes inside out and give the impression that they are not so much working as following a mission – the mission of proving that Polish cuisine is also innovative and by no means has to hide when comparing fine international dining.

The ambiance is appealing, even if, on arrival, you might initially be suspicious of whether the aforementioned mysterious address was the right one. Behind the entrance door, however, another world quickly opens up. The menu offers a straightforward selection of dishes chosen with love and care. Supposedly, a smaller menu speaks for higher quality and freshness, and here comes the proof. In addition, the menu is regularly adapted to the current season, which ensures you won't be bored with the dishes, even with repeated visits.

While the restaurant's location in a remote industrial complex on the outskirts of the city is no longer a secret, visitors to Wrocław are still strongly recommended to embark on this adventure. Even most of the higher-priced restaurants around the market square don't come close to the quality of food offered here.

47 The Naked Swordsman
Somebody lost his clothes while gambling...

🗺 D

🚩 Plac Uniwersytecki 🚇 Uniwersytet Wrocławski 🕐 All year round
🔴 Fontanna Szermierza ⏭ Of course you'll have to admire the wonderful University building 92

When you enter the historic old town from the north through the university gate, you'll see the statue of a naked man, beautifully illuminated in the evening. It was erected in 1901-1904 by Hugo Lederer, later a professor at the Berlin Academy of Fine Arts. But what exactly is this statue all about?

According to legend, the young man depicted here drank a little too much while playing cards – apparently so much that his cognitive abilities suffered, and he lost his entire fortune while gambling. But not only that: even his clothes are said to have served as a wager at the end. He was only allowed to keep his weapon – a foil – as a symbol of honour and a gesture of mercy. Sadly, today's drunken thieves are less merciful, as the *Säbeljürge* – as the statue was called during German times – has had his foil stolen several times.

Some claim that the figure is Hugo Lederer, who came to Wrocław because he was lured by the sculptor Christian Behrens. Unfortunately, the truth of this legend can no longer be verified. In any case, the figure has become the university's trademark, and all publications feature a drawing of it. Especially in winter, the city's inhabitants take loving care of their fencer – on cold days, he likes to wear a cap, a scarf, or even boxer shorts. Interestingly, there is even a replica of the statue in Leverkusen, Germany.

Today, this magnificent Art Nouveau sculpture is regarded as a memorial reminding us of the possible consequences of increased alcohol consumption. Is it just a coincidence that it is located directly in front of the university's main building?

48 The Narrow-gauge Railway Station
*A somewhat unusual railway station –
in timber-framed style*

🚆 Plac Staszica 4a 🚇 Plac Staszica 🕐 All year round 🍷 Dawny dworzec kolejki wąskotorowej 🌐 kleinbahn.pl ⏩ The Old City Port is not far away from here **58**

Wrocław is not only a city of bridges but a city of railway stations. The narrow-gauge railway station is not a regular station anymore and used to be the starting point for a narrow-gauge railway line. From today's Plac Staszica (formerly *Benderplatz* in German times), it was possible to travel to Trzebnica on the „small railway" from 1898 onwards.

The popular destination in the Cat's Mountains made the route very popular for weekend escapes, especially as the journey on the cute train was a great experience. Even today, the natural areas in the north of Wrocław are great places to experience nature, such as the Barycz Valley Landscape Park – a paradise for bird lovers. Unfortunately, the station had to give way to the increasing car traffic – it was first rebuilt and finally closed down in 1967. Perhaps this was partially driven by the fact that after various accidents involving the narrow-gauge railway, the speed was limited to 10 km/h within the city (and only 30 km/h was usual outside towns). The speed could hardly compete with getting there, even by bicycle.

The building is fascinating: it is an old, well-preserved timber-framed house that you probably wouldn't recognise as a railway station unless you spotted the remains of the tracks and the train model hidden behind the fence.

As seen from the large wooden crucifix on the site, the church administration now owns the property. And while you are there, there is a huge memorial in the immediate vicinity for the „Soviet hell" victims who were deported to Siberia. With these clear words, the Polish, Russian, and German inscriptions express the pain of the people who suffered this fate.

49 The National Forum of Music

As long as the music is loud enough when the world ends!

Plac Wolności 1 — Narodowe Forum Muzyki
All year round — Narodowe Forum Muzyki — nfm.wroclaw.pl
» Continue to explore culture at OP ENHEIM **62**

Freedom Square *(Plac Wolności)* in Wrocław looked like many things about 15 years ago, but certainly not like freedom. It was used as a huge car park near the city centre, and little of its original splendour was left. So it was probably a great idea when the city planners decided to move the car park underground to make room for something new.

In 2010-2015, the National Music Forum was built, an impressive masterpiece of modern architecture. Every detail, no matter how small, has been designed to ensure the best possible quality of sound. The chairs were designed to not affect the sound, whether occupied or not. Even the stage is adjustable to ensure optimal acoustics depending on the style of music. In the large concert hall, which fits up to 1800 guests, the ceiling has been fitted with movable plaster elements to avoid any excessive vibration. A double wall ensures no outside noise can disrupt the musicians. In the hall, even the end of the world might go unnoticed by concertgoers.

The outside of the building was, of course, designed with a vision in mind – the wooden elements of the facade are meant to be reminiscent of violins, and the elements in black and white are meant to be reminiscent of a piano. All these details make the National Forum of Music one of the best concert halls in Poland. Experiencing a concert in such a setting is already worth the journey to Wrocław.

After a lengthy construction process that brought some surprises, such as archaeological discoveries and groundwater intrusion, it is also one of the most expensive concert halls in the country.

A lot has happened on the grounds of the former car park. A huge, albeit not particularly green, forecourt has been created, which attracts many skateboarders, inline skaters, cyclists, and e-scooter riders. In winter, the square has a special charm – snowmen are crafted by kids, and a colourful „I love Wrocław" installation invites everyone to take some snowy photos.

50 The Nawa Sculpture
A dinosaur skeleton in the city centre?

- Wyspa Daliowa 🚇 Hala Targowa 🕐 All year round 🚩 Nawa 🌐 zieta.pl
- Don't miss Słodowa Island just next to it – relax in the countless floating bars during summer or take great pictures of the illuminated University from there **81**

At first glance, it resembles an imitation of a dinosaur skeleton that could hardly be more modern. The so-called „Nawa sculpture" was made with the help of the new FIDU (Freie Innendruckumformung or free inner pressure forming) technology. The creator of the giant open-air sculpture, Oskar Zięta, developed this production process himself during his studies at ETH Zurich. The process's upside is that bionic forms can be efficiently produced.

The sculpture is the first large-scale work of this kind to be created using FIDU technology and is intended to inspire future architectural projects. The 35 steel arches were inflated with compressed air in a former shipyard to create the desired curvatures. The design is inspired by the immediate surroundings of the location. With the Ossolineum, the church tower on Sand Island, and the Market Hall, the sculpture takes various forms from these surroundings and perfectly adapts them. Incidentally, the name „Nawa" means something like „nave". If steel could grow naturally like a tree, the result would, in all likelihood, look relatively similar. A fascinating feature for viewers is the light reflection that makes the construction appear different from every angle. The interior of the object also offers an exciting perspective.

Since June 2017, the installation has been located on the once-dreary Daliowa Island, which has gained a lot of charm thanks to the more than 7500 newly planted flowers. The sculpture has received significant recognition in professional circles and leading architecture magazines and was nominated for the coveted Mies van der Rohe Award. Further details, including the production process, are available on the artist's extensive website.

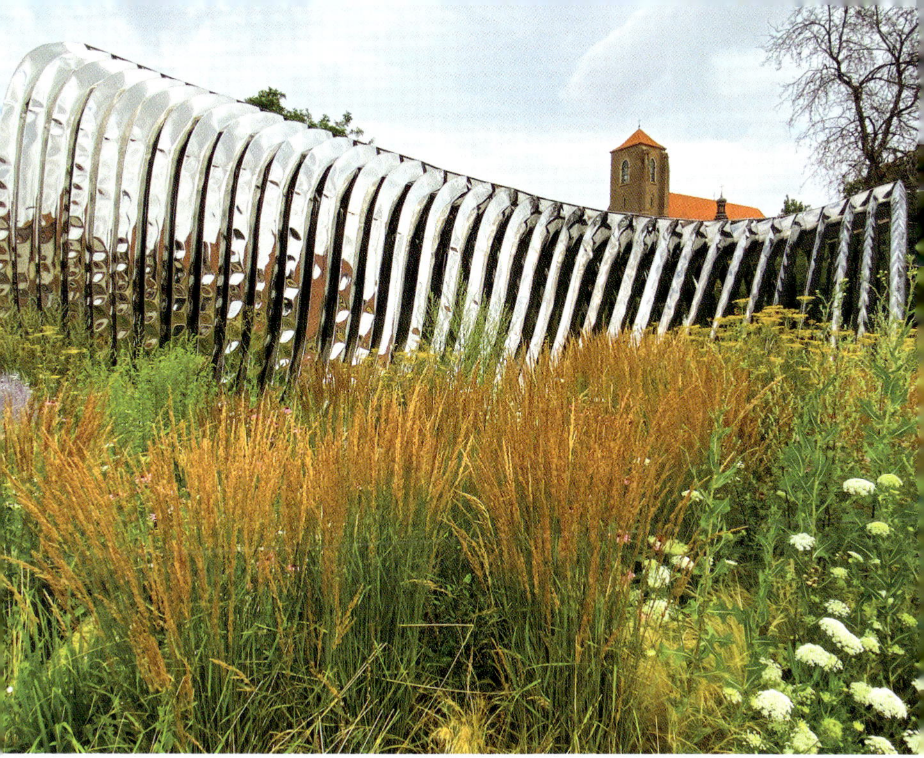

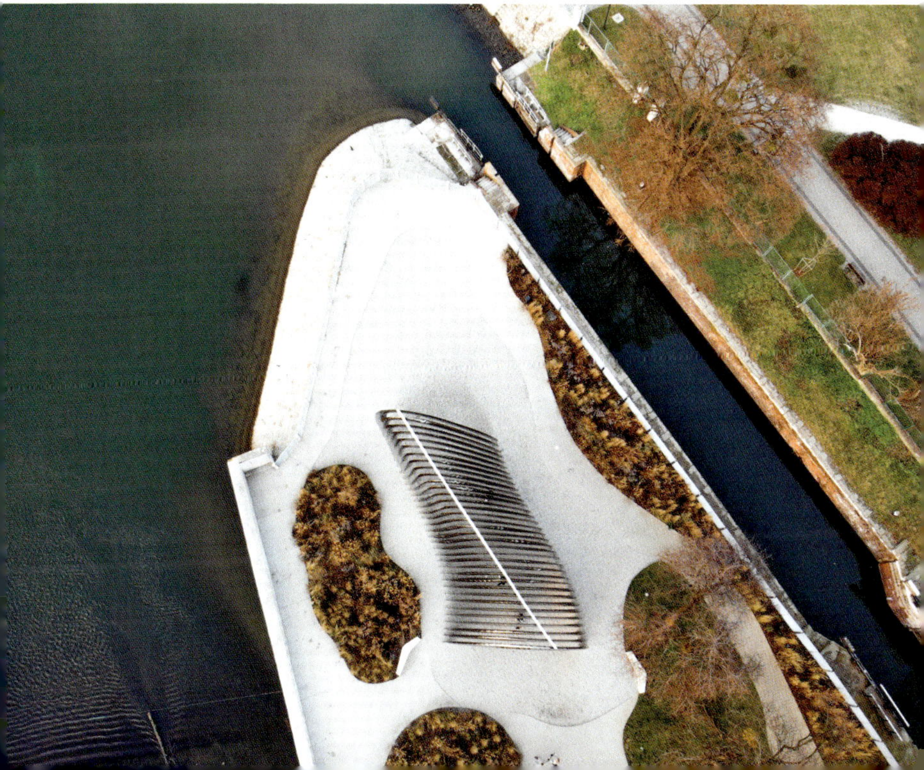

51 The Neighborhood of Brochów
Train tracks, a maze, and tropical fruits...

B

• Wrocław Brochów • All year round • Brochów
» Return to the fairytale castle of Wrocław's Main Railway Station 97

This one is for the more advanced Wrocław visitor: even the average Wrocław resident might be unaware of the great hornbeam maze within the city limits. This dream of every drone photographer can be found in Brochów, on the Eastern outskirts of the city. Children have particular fun disappearing and getting lost in the maze, but the unknown labyrinth is only a tiny part of what makes Brochów a district worth exploring further.

Despite it being an area where few tourists stray, there are some superlatives to be found, including Wrocław's oldest park, Brochowski Park. This beautiful park was created by the Augustinian canons, who owned the place then, in the early 18th century (from 1727).

You wouldn't believe it, but until 1749, there was even a „pineapple house" in Brochów, which has since been demolished. But it is interesting to know that the delicious tropical fruit was already cultivated in 1702. Who would have suspected such exotic things in Wrocław?

And as so often in this city, many places have a strong connection to the past. Brochów experienced a memorable event in 1842 when the first Silesian railway line was opened from Wrocław to Oława. About 50 years later, in 1896, the largest marshalling yard in Central Eastern Europe opened its doors on the same site. To this day, it is one of the most important freight stations in Poland. It is, therefore, no surprise that Brochów has developed into a classic railway town and its population increased by as much as twenty times over a century.

So it's undoubtedly the right place for railway nostalgics, especially as the best railway dwarfs in town can be discovered there – the tiny bronze figures are by no means only to be found in the town centre.

52 The Neighborhood of Sępolno
A typical district or a big piece of art?

 B

🚇 Sępolno 🚊 Sępolno ⏰ All year round 🍴 Sępolno
» Find the eastern Centennial Stone 12

If you go to the east of the city and visit Sępolno, everything seems quite ordinary – a completely unspectacular, middle-class housing estate, as you know it, from every country in the world. What's the proverb again? Sometimes you can't see the forest for the trees. The unique charm of Sępolno only becomes apparent when you leave the forest of, in this case, houses.

You must climb to higher levels to grasp the overall piece of art. The city's viewpoints are ideal for those with good eyes: Sky Tower, the Elisabeth Church, or the Cathedral. Even better would be a motorised hang-glider flight or, if the flight route allows it, a view from the airplane window coming to Wrocław. Because from the air you can see the district is a huge model of the Silesian Eagle!

From 1919 to 1935, the district was built based on the role model of English garden cities to create more living space. Conveniently, the eagle is an important symbol in German and Polish cultures, so not much had to be changed in the transition after 1945...

For those interested in architecture, however, there's even more to discover in the immediate vicinity, namely the so-called „WuWa" (the German abbreviation for „Wohnungs- und Werkraumausstellung"). On the southwestern edge of Sępolno, a comprehensive model housing estate was built in just a few months in 1929. The buildings were intended to represent a future standard of living. And now they offer an impressive look at a vision of the future of housing from almost a century ago. At WUWAcafe at ul. Tramwajowa 2, you will not only find lots of information about this exhibition, but also tasty cakes and coffee.

You can also jump on a short bicycle tour – there's a city bike station next store. It's best to cycle through the settlement first, perhaps go a bit through the park and then proceed to the water. Along the Oder River, you can pass the zoo and some beach bars in the direction of the city centre. Enjoy!

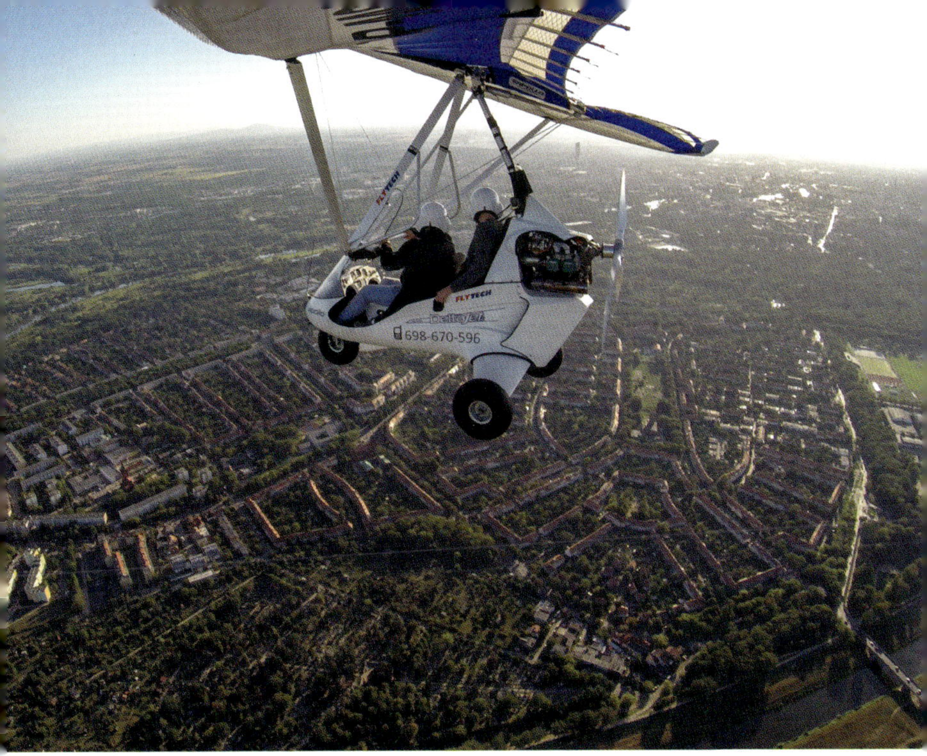
FLYTECH
698-670-596

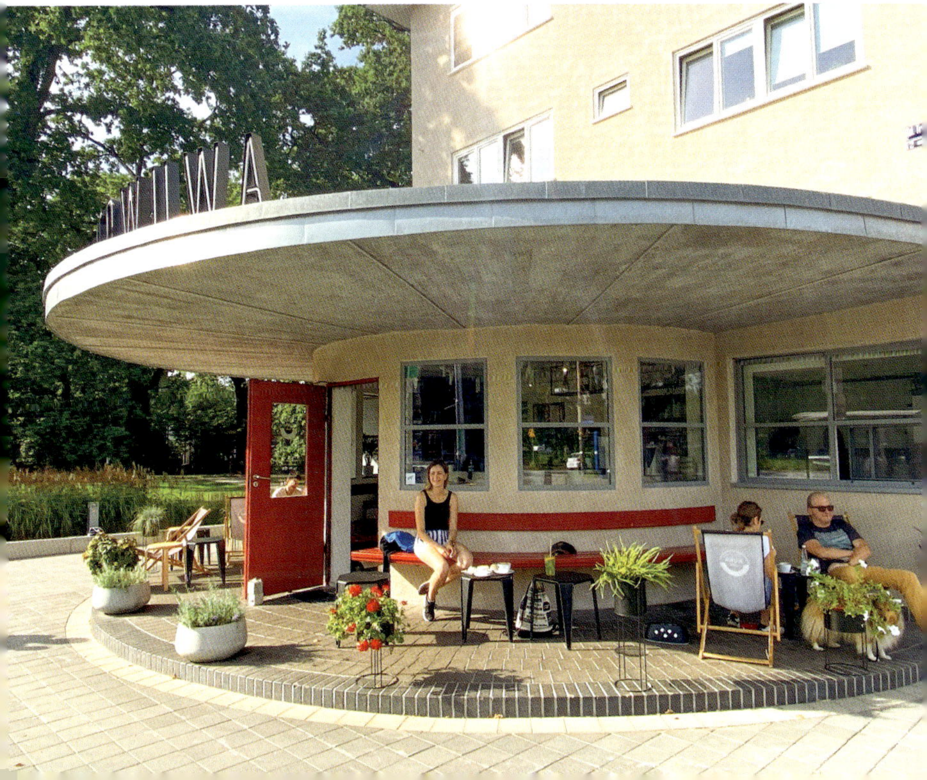

53 Neon Side Gallery
An unusual cemetery

 Ruska 46c Rynek All year round Galeria Neonów
How about a little bit of underground at the Square of John Paul II? **82**

It's been scientifically proven that people naturally tend to collect stuff. The classic objects of desire usually include coins, stamps, coasters, autographs, shoes, or postcards — handy things, in other words. In Wrocław, however, there is a more expansive example of a collector's love.

The story begins in 2005 in a pastry shop on ul. Nowowiejska. They advertised their cakes with a neon sign on the facade, but this advertisement suddenly disappeared one day. A passing lawyer named Tomasz Kosmalski noticed and asked the owner out of curiosity. The confectioner confirmed that the neon sign was destined for scrapping and had been dismantled. Kosmalski did not hesitate and bought it for exactly 100 zloty.

But what do you do with a big neon sign bought on the spot?

First, you hide it in the cellar and let it collect dust. But suddenly, more and more neon signs disappeared from the facades of Wrocław, and the private collection in Kosmalski's cellar kept growing. It, therefore, seems only logical that Kosmalski set up a foundation called „Neon Side" and started the quest for a place to present his collection to the public. In an interview, he said that it should not gather dust in a museum but rather should be visible on the street for everybody – a little hint to the Neon Museum in Warsaw.

And he found the best possible place: a courtyard on ul. Ruska, where the company „Reklama" had produced neon signs for Lower Silesia for 50 years. Today, numerous works are exhibited there – some coming in at a weight of even 400 kilograms. In 2019, the courtyard was renovated and now displays various works of street art in addition to the neon gallery.

A piece of alternative and artistic Wrocław was created there, and it's hard to imagine the cityscape without it. The installations are often lovingly referred to as the „neon cemetery." It's no surprise that this cemetery has become one of the most popular picture spots in Wrocław.

54 The New Market Square

A counter-design to the Market Square and the Salt Market Square

🚩 Plac Nowy Targ 🚌 Plac Nowy Targ 🕐 All year round
🅿 Plac Nowy Targ ❱❱ Visit the picturesque Gondola Bay **23**

The New Market Square *(Plac Nowy Targ)* is where the German history of Wrocław began: the first German settlement was mentioned here in 1214. As with the historic market square, the square was probably delineated after the Mongol invasion of 1241. Unfortunately, the Neptune Fountain, erected in 1732 and marked the middle of the square, was destroyed in the Second World War and has now disappeared. Due to space issues, more and more market stalls had to be moved from the Market Square to the New Market Square over the years, as there was a veritable crowd of sellers – at times, there were 30 stalls selling herring there alone.

If you search for historical photos online and compare them with today's status of the big concrete square, you will quickly realise the tragedy that took place: 99 percent of the market was destroyed during the war. Only two buildings survived the last months of the war – the municipal office in the south of the square and a corner building on the north side of ul. Jodłowa.

Instead of a cautious reconstruction as performed with Salt Market Square, it was decided to erect typical post-war buildings in the modernist style – a consequence of the pressing housing need after the war. The once most important and largest weekly market in the city makes a dreary and sobering impression today, although the square was redeveloped a few years ago.

In winter, a brightly coloured Christmas tree provides a pleasant contrast. In the meantime, the city planners have granted the first licences to street food trucks to revitalise the square. There have also been several petitions for rebuilding the Neptune Fountain – unfortunately, without success yet. In any case, this place impressively shows one of the many different faces of Wrocław.

Wrocław's smallest café is also right next door: KIOSSO is just 2.65 square metres. Luckily, the owner Ahmed is an architect and was able to create his space in the best possible way.

55 The Night Market

When the mosquitoes buzz in summer, the Asian feeling is complete

- Tęczowa 65 🚊 Grabiszyńska
- May to September: Thu 17–0h, Fri 17–2h, Sat 15–2h, Sun 15–0h
- Nocny Targ Tęczowa 🌐 facebook.com/nocnytargteczowa
- Maybe move on to the greenhouse of Szklarnia? **86**

If you spend some time in Wrocław, you'll notice that in addition to the well-known and visible street markets, there are also many relatively small and alternative markets. These are often hidden in courtyards and are not immediately recognisable from the outside — the night market at ul. Tęczowa 65 is an excellent example of this, along with the EkoBazar mentioned earlier.

After passing through an inconspicuous gate at an old brick building, you are suddenly surrounded by the smell of Asian (and other) food stalls. The hipster-ish lights lead the way, and then you will find yourself in the middle of the night market. Many small stalls offer dishes from Thailand or Vietnam, as well as Mexican specialties or delicious empanadas from Argentina. The whole thing is completed by cool drinks perfect for a warm summer night.

Mosquito bites are not uncommon here either. After all, Wrocław is on the water. But maybe that's just part of a real night market – in any case, it brings back holiday memories of Southeast Asia.

The old factory building was once directly connected to the railway network. In an alternative-urban style, the outside area now features cosy upholstered armchairs and beach chairs that invite you to chill. The colourful lampshades, which have been converted into ceiling lamps, provide an ambience with a creative touch. There is a huge cultural programme here, as in so many places in Wrocław. Besides quiz nights, bingo games, concerts, and open-air cinema, dance lessons are also on the schedule.

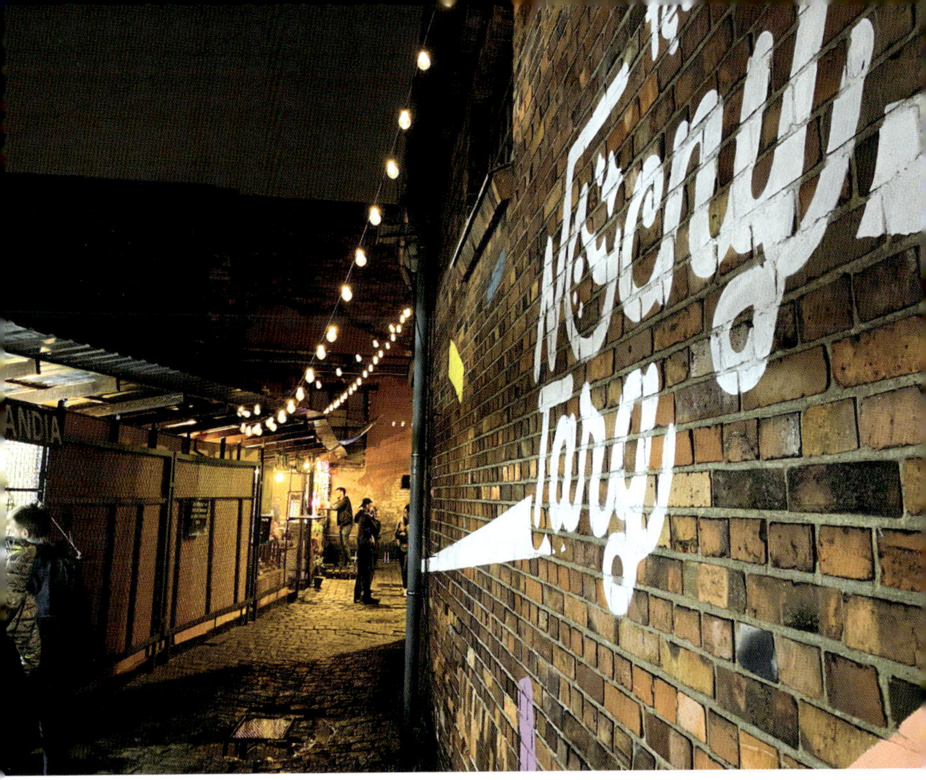

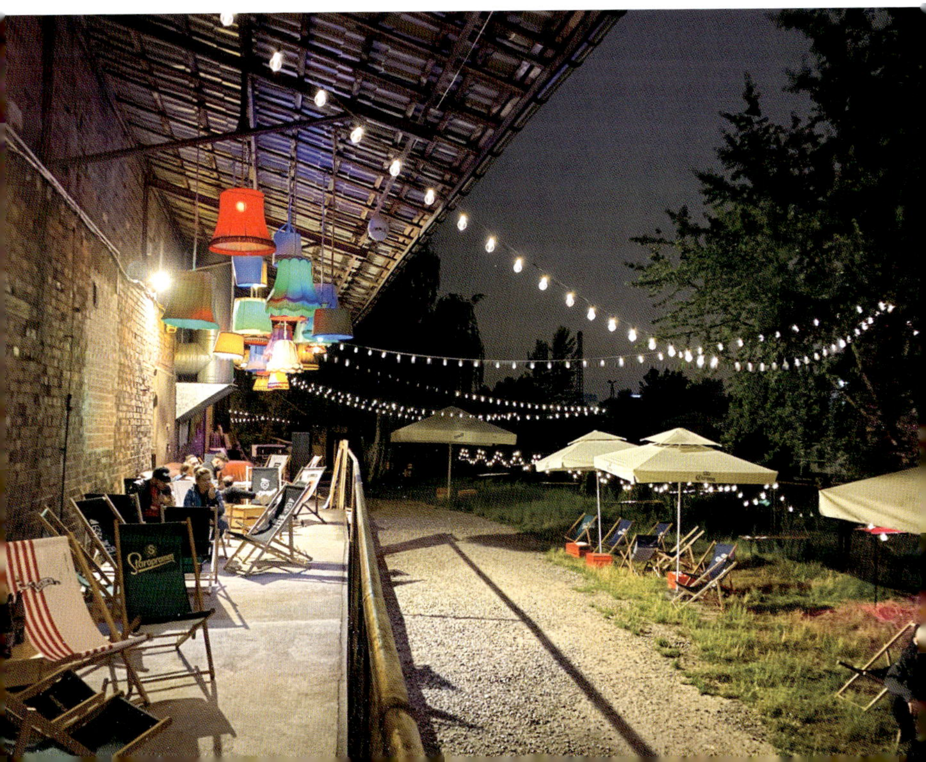

56 The Oder River Banks

🗺 B,E *Why go to the seaside?*

🚏 Pasterska 🚌 Mosty Warszawskie or Karłowice 🕐 All year round
🚊 Stara Odra ⏩ During the summer season you can't miss out on the numerous beach bars along the river! **3**

If one element is closely associated with Wrocław, it's clearly water. It is an integral part of the city, and a Wrocław without the Oder River would simply be incomplete. But in 1997, the inhabitants' love for their river was tested – the year of the tragic Millennium Flood.

Of course, the people of Wrocław hold no resentments, and the banks of the Oder River continue to be a popular destination for day trips, especially in summer. The recently developed cycle paths invite bikers to tour in the partial shade of the trees, families with and without kids enjoy the fresh air beyond the ring roads, and students like to enjoy a cold lemonade on picnic blankets. Alcohol in public is generally prohibited – there are only a few places with exceptions and the banks on the Oder Rivers aren't one of them!

However, for the vast majority of Poles, there is no reason to set aside their plans for a short holiday when it's right at their doorstep. In almost any weather, you will observe the secret national sport: fishing! After all, what could be better than putting a fresh catch on the barbecue right next to the river? On hot days, a few people are even tempted to jump into the cool water.

If you are visiting Wrocław as part of a city trip and would like to experience a bit of nature, you have a wonderful option: there are rental stations for so-called „city bikes" (WRM) on almost every corner of the city. The first twenty minutes are free, and even after, the prices are still very affordable. The best way to combine a trip along the banks of the Oder River is with a visit to the Centennial Hall, the Olympic Stadium, and Szczytnicki Park. For a little break, get ice cream or coffee at Mała Czarna – a local coffee roastery located a few kilometres away from the city centre and a hidden gem.

57 Odra Centrum

Science, a living room, and a workbench in one place

- Wybrzeże J. Słowackiego 5B ❖ Urząd Wojewódzki (Impart)
- Mon–Fri 8:30–21h, Sat–Sun 10–21h ❖ odracentrum.org
- Odra Centrum ❯❯ You will most likely see the Grunwaldzki Bridge **24**

Who doesn't dream of owning a houseboat? The only problem is that, at least for most of us, the results – after hours of research – are always the same: it's too complicated, bureaucratic, and expensive. And so the dream remains as such. But this is not the case with Kamil Zaremba, because he decided to move his residence to the water out of his love for the Oder River. And for this to happen, he put up with years of complicated official procedures.

However, his commitment was not limited to the houseboat he moved into in 2013: as chairman of the OnWater Foundation, with other water-loving Wrocław residents, he put the „Odra Centrum" project together. You could say this is just another houseboat, but much larger, as the Odra Centrum hosts a floating learning and cultural centre. Here, children, entire school classes, and adults can expand their knowledge about various subjects. Here you can learn knot-tying techniques or acquire special know-how for water photography. You can also do handicraft techniques like pottery, macramé, and tie-dye. And if you think there is nothing modern here, the 3D printing and robotics programming courses are worth a try. At the kayak rental, also offered, you get one hour for free if you get active and fish some rubbish out of the Oder River.

Another big plus: if you don't feel like taking a workshop, you can make yourself comfortable in the Odra Café with Lucy, the house dog, and enjoy the view of the water with a book from the extensive library (with many books related to water and Wrocław, of course), and, in summer, from the roof terrace. The walls are decorated with private collections of old Wrocław postcards, city maps, and barometers. The dream of a houseboat can hardly come true more cheaply than here.

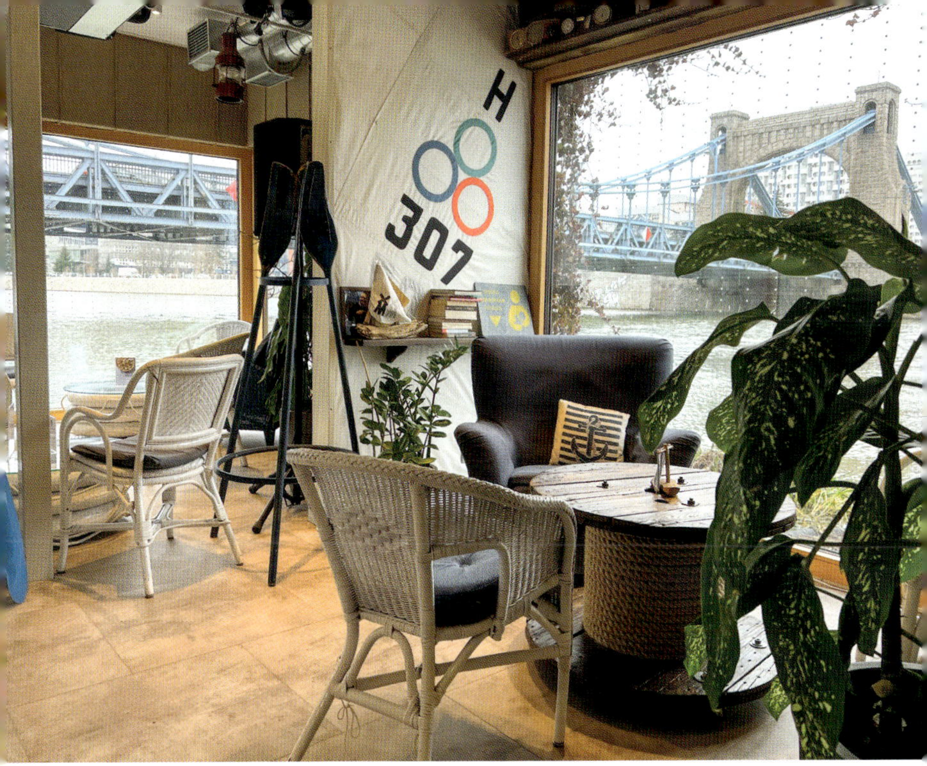
H
307

NAUCZYCIELE
w każdy
wtorek
KAWA GRATIS

CAFE/KAJAK/LODY
odra

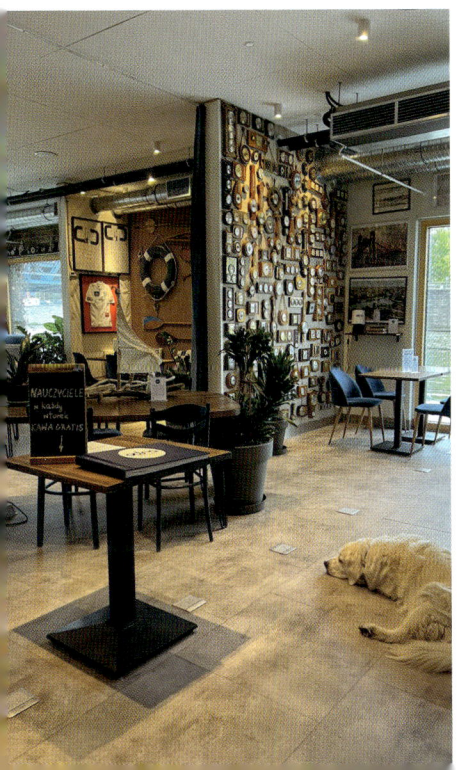

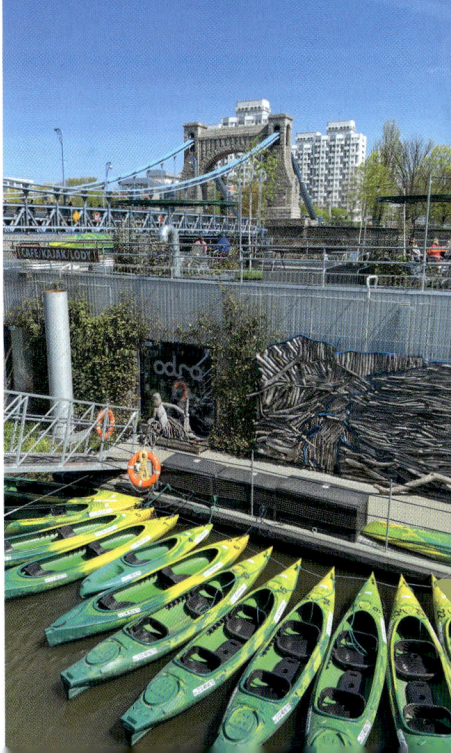

58 The Old City Port

A *paradise for urbex photographers and Instagrammers*

🔴 Kleczkowska 52 🚊 Kleczkowska 🕐 All year round ⛔ Port Miejski
⏩ Find out what Macondo is all about 34

As early as the Middle Ages, Wrocław offered good loading and unloading facilities for ships with the Oder River running through the city. In 1842, when the railway was inaugurated in Wrocław, there were also plans to open up a port facility with a railway connection.

In 1868, a small, provisional port was built with such a connection, but it quickly reached its capacity limits. So in 1880, it was decided to invest in a modern port, and the idea of the municipal commercial port *(Port Miejski)* was sealed. However, the detailed planning proved difficult, so construction could only begin 17 years later. With its completion in 1901, Wrocław finally had a city port that was already geared towards maximum efficiency. With the increasing popularity of the railway, however, the traffic of goods shifted more and more from water to rail.

Today, a large part of the port is not in use and serves as a parking space for damaged ships or as a buffer zone in winter. There are no longer any actual port operations, although many of the facilities, such as the 70-metre-long coal conveyor belt, the customs office, and various cranes, are still in place. The remaining buildings are mostly rented out to local companies as storage and production space. Thanks to its industrial charm, the port is becoming increasingly popular with the urbex and photography scene. Some of the disused buildings show clear signs of decay, and the combination with the harbour basin, railway tracks, cranes, and rotting ships makes the whole area a perfect place for all sorts of lenses. Occasionally, semi-legal events take place there, such as small concerts and art projects by the alternative scene.

Visiting the port is a little journey back to the turn of the century – an absolute must for all photographers and Instagrammers. Before the local real estate mafia snatches up this last great plot of land and builds expensive condominiums, that is.

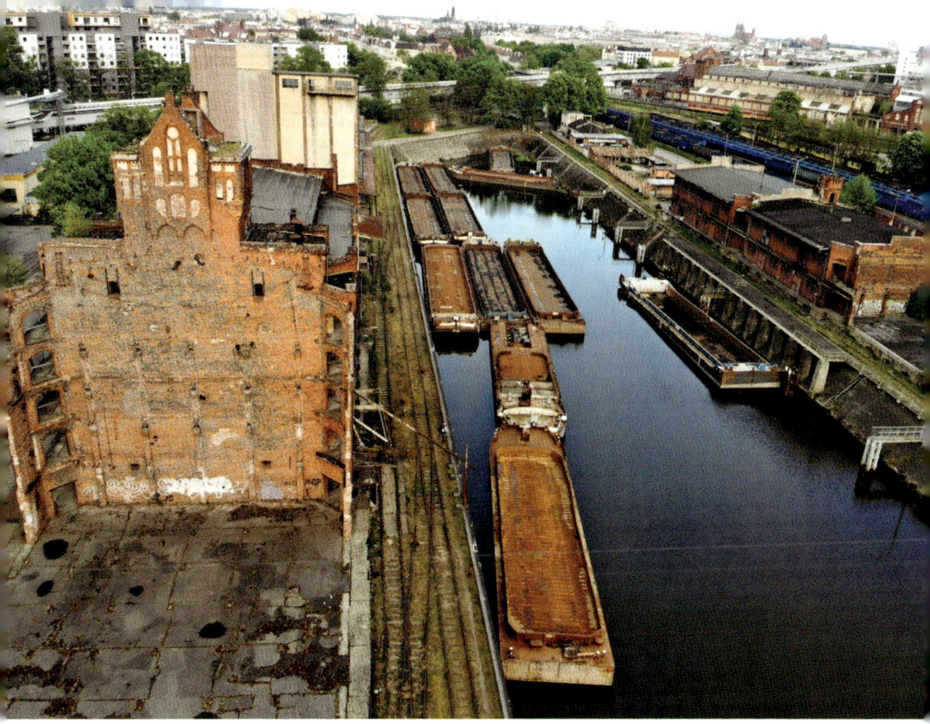

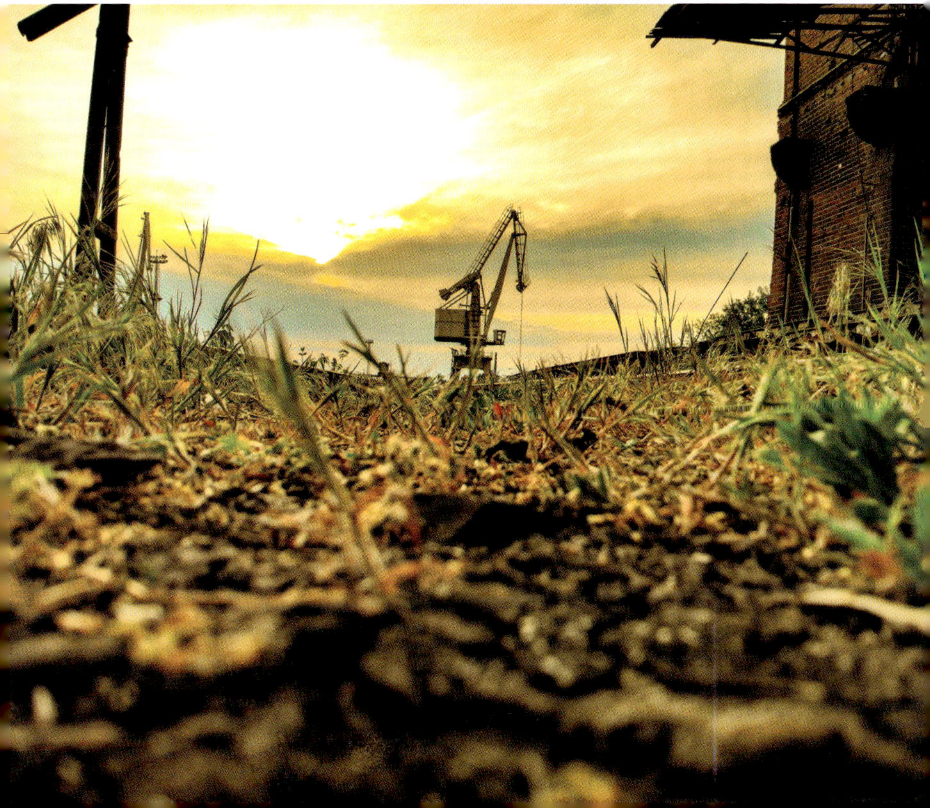

59 The Old Guardhouse
A roof terrace and the most beautiful weather station in the city

🅕 Świdnicka 38A 🚇 Renoma 🕒 Daily 8–21h, Sat–Sun until 22h
☕ Cafe Borówka 🌐 blueberryroasters.pl ⏩ Just around the corner: The National Forum of Music **49**

In the past, the Świdnicka Gate had guarded the entrance to the city at this spot, but today only the old guardhouse remains at ul. Świdnicka 38A, indicating where the entrance to the city once stood. It was probably built in the 19th century as a memorial to the former gate.

Over time, the historic building has been transformed into one of the many extraordinary places in Wrocław. In addition to a small art gallery on the ground floor, you'll find Café Borówka. One should not be deceived by the relatively minimalist interior: the special charm of this place is revealed as soon as you climb the stairs and step onto one of Wrocław's most beautiful roof terraces – a wonderful spot to read a book in peace or simply enjoy the lovely view. By the way, the view is constantly being „updated": previously, the view was towards the monument to Kaiser Wilhelm I – which was removed in 1945 and replaced in 2007 by a monument to Bolesław I, the first Polish king.

It should be noted that Bolesław I followed all relevant coronavirus rules in 2020 and wore a mask. And sometimes on cold winter days, he wears a scarf. Like the naked swordsman, it seems that Wrocław residents like to dress up their monuments.

The squeaky green plastic chairs on the roof terrace harmonise perfectly with the greenery of the Old Town promenade, and the view of the Renoma department store. The entire surrounding area has a certain magic vibe that's especially worth recommending in spring, just as the first warm rays of sunlight fall on the city. It's not uncommon for visitors to drop in for a quick cup of coffee, spontaneously make new acquaintances, and then suddenly realise that half the day had already passed.

Those who were able to break free from the spell of the roof terrace will find the city's most beautiful weather station in front of the building – Róża Wiatrów. It has been in service faithfully for more than 130 years, and its design certainly bears comparison with the new-fangled digital displays.

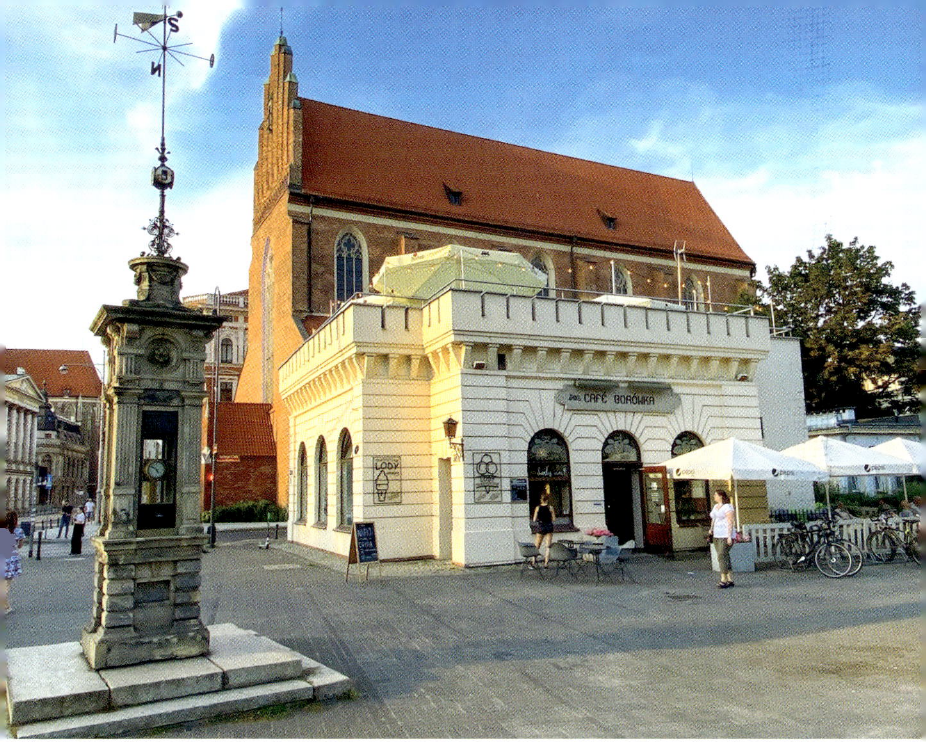
CAFÉ BOROWKA
LODY

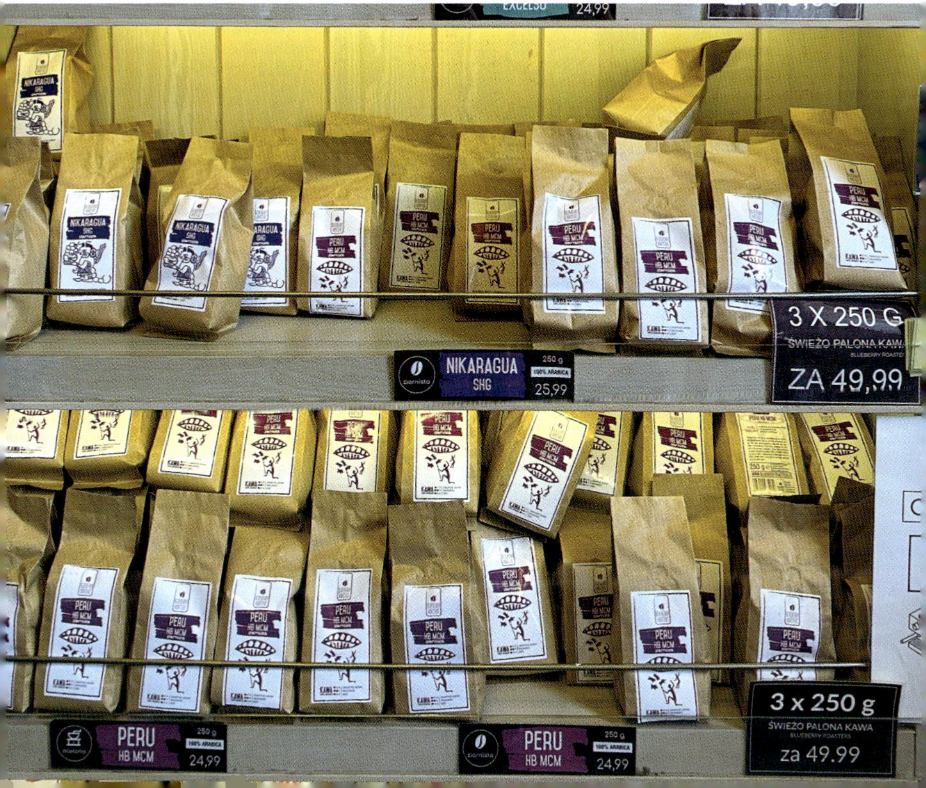
EXCELSO 24,99
NIKARAGUA SHG
ziarnista
NIKARAGUA SHG 250 g 100% ARABICA 25,99
3 X 250 G
ŚWIEŻO PALONA KAWA
BLUEBERRY ROASTERS
ZA 49,99
mielona
PERU HB MCM 250 g 100% ARABICA 24,99
ziarnista
PERU HB MCM 250 g 100% ARABICA 24,99
3 x 250 g
ŚWIEŻO PALONA KAWA
BLUEBERRY ROASTERS
za 49.99

60 The Old Jewish Cemetery
A quiet sound in a fairytale place

- Ślężna 37/39
- Uniwersytet Ekonomiczny
- Daily 11–17h
- Stary Cmentarz Żydowski
- muzeum.miejskie.wroclaw.pl
- Have a walk to the water tower **94**
- Free admission on Thursdays

Traces of history are visible in many places in Wrocław, not only on monuments or commemorative plaques – in fact, the whole merging of the city creates this unique atmosphere. The Old Jewish Cemetery is one of the best examples of a place where time seems to have stood still.

For decades after the war, the cemetery was left alone. In 1975, it was recognised as an architectural monument, but it was not until 1984 that the maintenance and conservation of the cemetery began. Since its opening in 1856 (what was then *Lohestraße*), approximately 12,500 people have been buried there. As the elaborately designed graves and inscriptions reveal, most of the elite of that period – entrepreneurs, scientists, business owners, and politicians – were buried at this cemetery. With much pride, even the full job titles are often listed on the gravestones.

However, the peaceful chirping of birds and the tranquillity of the beautiful natural surroundings should not hide the tragic traces of the past: bullet holes from the Second World War are still visible in the walls surrounding the cemetery. The journey through time that begins when passing through the gates leads visitors into a ghost town where the silent echoes of fighting from the past can still be heard. Wrocław was once home to Germany's third-largest Jewish community.

The Old Jewish Cemetery has a connecting role in today's German-Polish relations as well: Since 1992, students from the Thomas Mann High School in Berlin have met annually with their counterparts from the ASSA High School in Wrocław and other volunteers to jointly care for the cemetery and contribute to its preservation. The project initiators, Dagmar Denzin and Eckhard Rieke, were awarded the Order of Merit of the Federal Republic of Germany in 2004.

The Old Mill Flea Market

Bicycle stolen? No worries, you might find it here!

🧭 Aleja Poprzeczna 33 🚏 Brücknera 🕒 Sundays 7–15h
🇵🇱 Targowisko MŁYN 🌐 facebook.com/TargnaMlynie
» Enjoy the Oder River Banks 56

The Sunday flea market at the old mill *(Targowisko Młyn)* is a worthwhile destination for families and bargain hunters. Located about two kilometres north of the Oder River, everything that can be sold is available there: in addition to fresh fruit and vegetables, you'll find scrap parts, boats, bicycles, plants and herbs, furniture, antiques, electrical parts, lawnmowers, records, and German board games. But the goods here are not the only reason why the flea market is so popular with the locals.

Especially early at sunrise, when the first bargain hunters arrive and quickly scour the semi-professionally set-up stalls for the best deals, there is a unique vibe. The moment when the sliding door of an old VW van suddenly opens and reveals itself to be a well-built salesroom is quite surprising. Above all, the place seems to have fallen out of time: it is easy to imagine that things were no different a few decades earlier.

Tourists usually don't venture this far out of the city centre, so this is an excellent opportunity to observe the real Sunday hustle and bustle of Wrocław. Residential visitors have even „recovered" their bicycles here, which were stolen a short time before in the city, and were then able to confront the seller in person to question where the bike came from. Thanks to situations like this, you might discover some free entertainment with a bit of luck.

If you can't make it to the flea market at the old mill, we recommend visiting a similar flea market at the former Świebodzki train station, which is a little closer to the city. *Plac Targowy Świebodzki* takes place on Sunday mornings too. Initially, you'll see a lot of clothes for sale, but the further you go, the more diverse it gets.

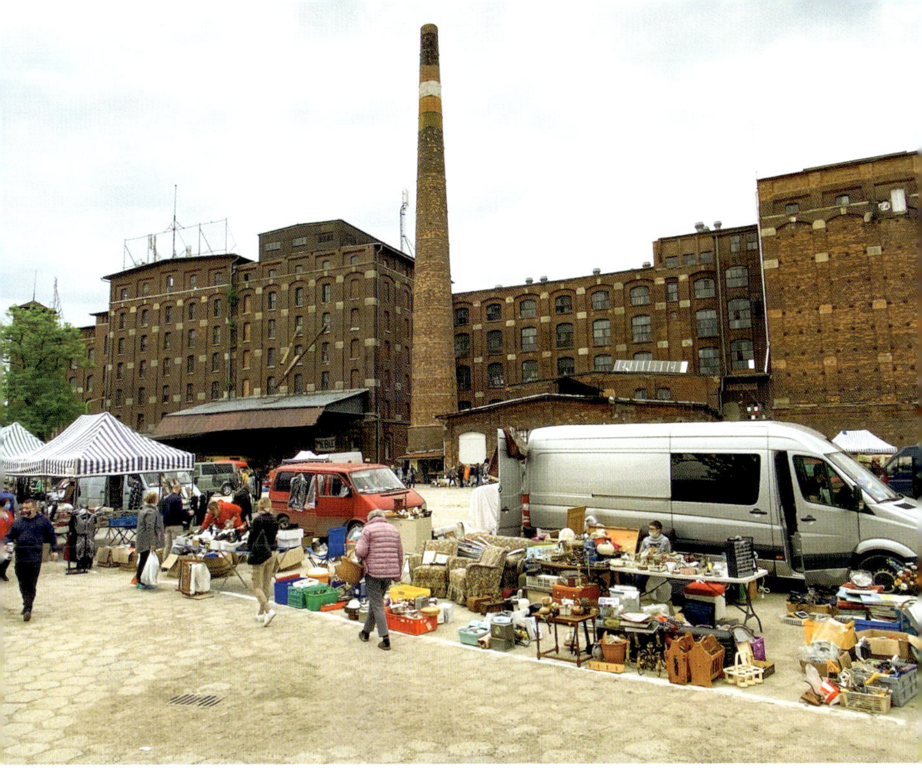

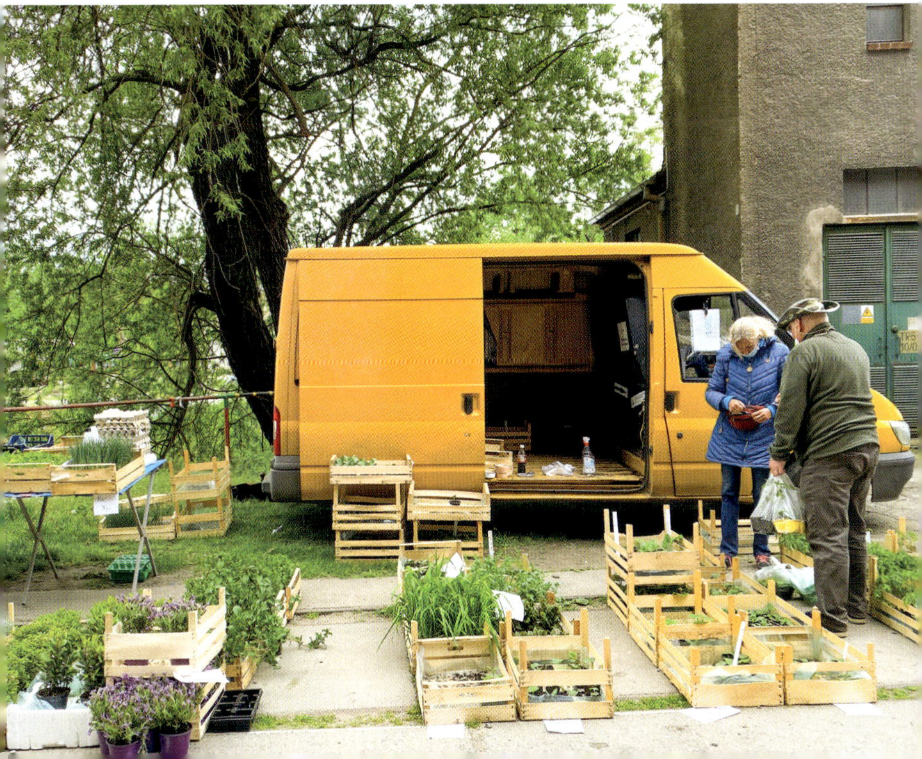

OP ENHEIM

An artistic bridge between Wrocław and Berlin

🏠 Plac Solny 4 🚇 Rynek 🕐 Wed + Thu 14–18h, Fri 14–19h, Sat + Sun 13–19h,
🌐 openheim.org 🔴 OP ENHEIM ⏩ See the Cinema New Horizons 14

„The real Berliner comes from Breslau," Kurt Tucholsky once said of Wrocław (using the previous German name), and the two cities are often compared. Indeed, there has always been a magical connection between Wrocław and Berlin, although this connection was severely broken during the Second World War and the subsequent westward shift of Poland.

Luckily some projects and initiatives are trying to move the two cities closer together. These include, for example, the culture train that has been connecting Berlin and Wrocław physically since 2016, and OP ENHEIM – a private art gallery opened in 2018 that seeks to establish a lasting connection between the two cities on an artistic level.

The Polish entrepreneur Violetta Wojnowski wanted to purchase one of the many old castles in need of renovation around Jelenia Góra, but decided to buy a „simple" house in the city centre before embarking on such an enormous adventure.

The old house – where the art gallery is – on the Salt Market Square was in poor condition and therefore received very little attention at the auction in 2012. In the last round, the only bidders had just withdrawn their bids, hoping to get the building even cheaper through negotiations. But at the very last minute, Wojnowski showed up – she hadn't found a parking space before – and made her spontaneous and successful surprise bid.

While the art gallery is unusual, so is the building itself. The house has an exciting history, about which almost nothing was known at the time of the purchase. The new owner then went out to search for clues, and in doing so, she discovered stories that she probably had not expected when she bought it. Lisa Höhenleitner has written a book on this, which is highly recommended.

A visit to the OP ENHEIM is also worthwhile for culinary reasons. Since 2019, the Młoda Polska bistro has been located on the ground floor. Beata Śniechowska is crafting modern interpretations of traditional Polish cuisine and is well known beyond the region since winning the Polish version of MasterChef.

63 Ossolineum Garden

An oasis of calm amidst the hustle and bustle of city life

- Zaułek Ossolińskich Uniwersytecka Daily 8–20h
- Barokowy ogród Ossolineum oss.wroc.pl
- Time for education - take the History Trail **28**

Wrocław is a city with a constant and dominant soundscape. The rattling vibration of the tram and its horn, which sounds more like a nostalgic telephone ringing, is a constant companion. On top of that are the unmistakable noises of cars rolling over cobblestones or amateur race drivers who mistake streets for racing tracks and start more sportily at the traffic lights. As lively as these sounds may seem from time to time, there are moments when you simply crave some sweet birds chirping and seek to enter an oasis of peace.

This is offered by the centrally located garden of the Ossolineum. The building which hosts the Ossolineum was built in 1690-1710 and was originally home to the Knights of the Cross with the Red Star – an order of knights with roots dating back to the 13th century, which was dedicated to fighting poverty and supporting the poorer members of society.

Today, the Ossolineum houses some valuable works of art, including drawings by Rembrandt and Dürer. And from a Polish point of view, there is one object that can probably be compared to the British Crown Jewels: the manuscript of Pan Tadeusz – the most famous work by the Polish poet Adam Mickiewicz. These treasures are kept in a special room under the highest security precautions and a constant temperature range of 14 to 18 degrees.

The garden of the Ossolineum was originally laid out in 1697 but didn't survive the centuries since. In its present form, the garden has only existed since 2007, and before that, the area was used as a sports field.

This green space is one of the most beautiful in the city. Spending just a few minutes on a park bench there calms the mind and recharges your batteries. Surprisingly, the garden attracts only a few groups of tourists, whereas happy couples dominate there. The view of the St. Matthew Church next door, a Gothic gem, completes the painting-like scenery.

○ And if you walk around the corner, you'll find Café Cherubinowy Wędrowiec right in the garden. What could be better than enjoying a cappuccino in these beautiful, relaxed surroundings?

64 Palace Pawłowice

The most beautiful arboretum in the city

📍 Pawłowicka 87/89 🚉 Wrocław Pawłowice 🕐 All year round
⛔ Pałac Kornów w Pawłowicach ⏩ Get back to the city centre and hunt some dwarfs 19

This wonderful castle, built in 1891 in the French Neo-Renaissance style based on a design by architect August Orth, often doesn't get the attention it deserves. For decades, the building was owned by the von Schweinichen family, an old noble Silesian family that still has active descendants today.

In 1886, Heinrich von Korn bought up the entire village of Pawelwitz, as it used to be called. He had the necessary money as the publisher and editor of the Silesian Newspaper and owner of a paper factory, and he founded the Silesian Museum on the side. Towards the end of the 19th century, he handed the castle over to his daughter Maria and son-in-law Konstantin von Schweinichen. The coat of arms of the von Korns still adorns the castle together with that of his wife (Helena von Moriz-Eichborn), despite its expropriation in 1945.

One of the absolute highlights is the park surrounding the castle. It's an arboretum – a collection of different and exotic trees and shrubs that cover 70 hectares. The Gloriette there is a perfect picture spot for wedding couples, but it's also very much appreciated by all other visitors. Thanks to the city center's distance, the visitors' crowds are limited, although the park is open to the public. It takes about 45 minutes by bike – an ideal half-day trip to make.

Today, the property belongs to the University of Environmental and Life Sciences, which maintains an experimental facility and training centre. But the castle can be booked for conferences, trainings, and other events. Last but not least, the restaurant located outside the castle is certainly worth a visit.

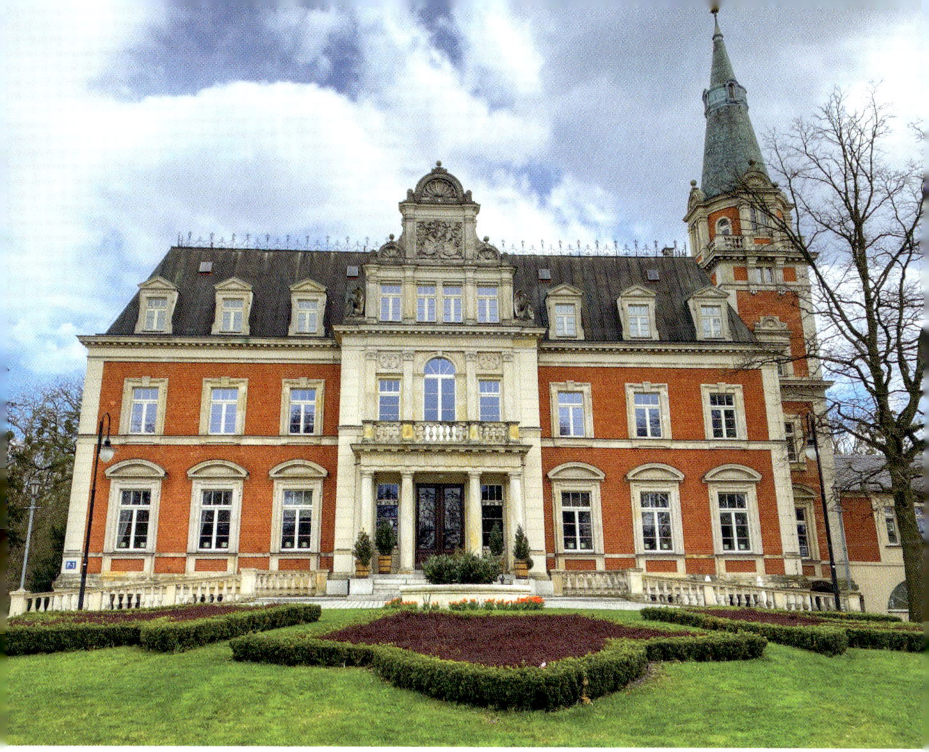

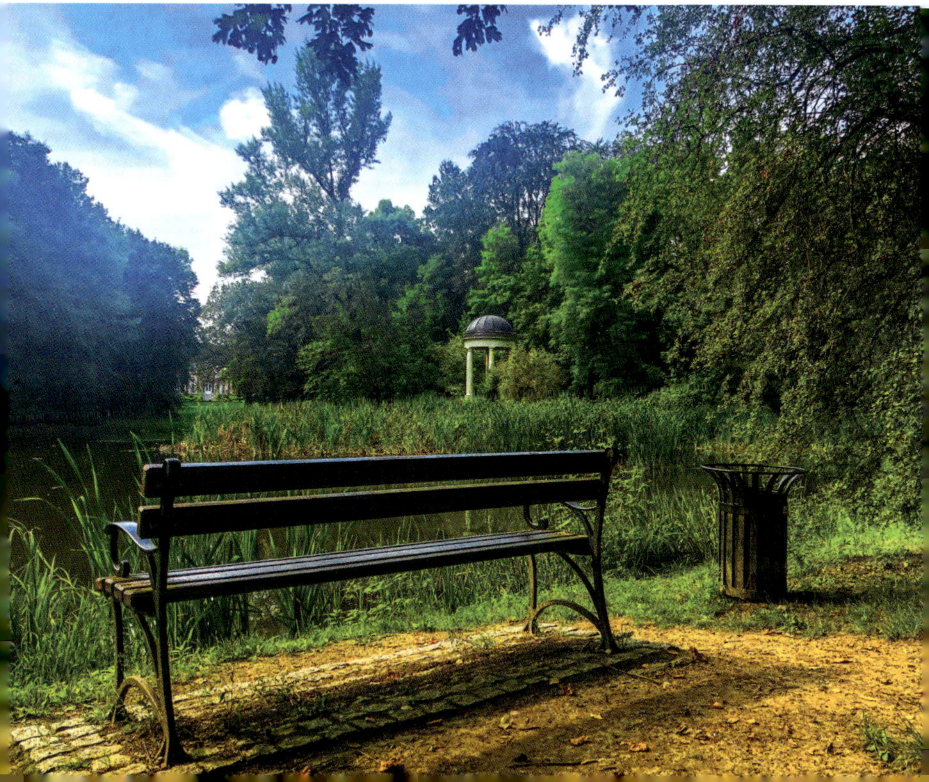

65 Parrot Coffee

Some people bring dogs to their workplace, others bring parrots

Generała Józefa Bema 2 | Plac Bema | Mon–Fri 7:45–20h, Sat+Sun 10–20h | Parrot Coffee | facebook.com/ParrotCoffeeWro
» Explore Cathedral Island at sunset to meet the lamplighter 10

In recent years, more and more small cafés with special stories or interesting unique selling points have opened in Wrocław. Parrot Coffee is undoubtedly one of them! Cat cafés, on the other hand, are an almost forgotten trend in Wrocław (although there is still one!).

At first glance, you might think it's just a colourful café with a jungle design. That is, of course, until you see Jon and Pablo, the two parrots who round off the vintage hipster jungle parade inside their lovely toy-filled aviary – the part-time home for the café's two talkative protagonists.

It is not uncommon for intense philosophical discussions between friends to be suddenly interrupted by one of the feathered friends with a loud and determined „Arrrgh!". It should be noted that the parrots have an impressive vocabulary of around 400 words, but only in Polish – one of the most difficult languages in the world! Animal rights activists may fear that parrots are only kept there simply for commercial purposes, but don't worry: the owner of the café, Mateusz, grew up with parrots, and the mutual love is easy to spot. He simply brings his pets to work with him – just like other people bring dogs.

The cosy vintage chairs and the green jungle atmosphere form a wonderful contrast to the clear glass design of the office building, where the café is located on the ground floor. In addition to the standard coffee selection, there are specialty coffees available such as Chemex, AeroPress, and freshly brewed drip coffee from different origins.

Parrot Coffee has expanded recently. A second branch opened near the Galeria Dominikańska shopping mall. It's safe to assume that the parrots will soon regard Wrocław as their natural habitat.

66 Partisan Hill

After a long legal battle, a future is finally in sight again

⊙ Piotra Skargi 18 🚇 Wzgórze Partyzantów 🕐 All year, but it might still be not accessible 🚏 Wzgórze Partyzantów ⏩ Walk along the City Moat (Old Town Promenade) **15**

Many old buildings in the town followed a certain post-war life cycle. This began with (partial) destruction, and if reconstruction didn't take place, natural decay set in – often followed by demolition – as was the case of Wrocław's second market hall. Other old buildings, such as the All Saints' Hospital, have been expensively converted into luxury apartments. And there are still properties that remain in long-term hibernation with uncertain fates – including Partisan Hill.

It is a belvedere based on an idea by the brothers Gustav and Adolf Liebich. These merchants were involved in founding the first Lower Silesian sugar factory, which paved the way for their wealth. Unfortunately, Gustav died unexpectedly, but this only strengthened Adolf's commitment to the realisation of the Belvedere. He donated the then considerable sum of 70,000 thalers for its construction. In comparison to that, the city's annual budget of 30,000 thalers at the time seemed downright small.

The vision of a magnificent local recreation area was realised by the architect Karl Schmidt in 1867 and Partisan Hill was ceremoniously opened in the same year. In a very short time, it developed into one of the city's most popular meeting places. Concerts and other cultural events and a beer garden certainly provided many remarkable moments. In bad weather, the colonnade offered shelter, and in winter, an ice-skating rink was set up.

In the 19th century, the most beautiful Silesian belvedere was considered by many travel guides to be the main attraction of Wrocław. Unfortunately, the former lookout tower was blown up during wartime and can now only be admired in old photos. The German name „Liebichshöhe" is, of course, a nod to its financier – the city unceremoniously renamed the former pocket bastion, which was part of the city fortifications until the surrender to Napoleon in 1807. It is also worth mentioning that Liebich waived the rent for the benefit of the city – apparently true altruism, which earned him the title of honorary citizen of the city.

In 1990, under sketchy circumstances, a 40-year lease was agreed to a private investor. In this agreement, he was obliged to restore the building. However, after nothing happened, the matter ended up in court, but it was not until 2017 that the city administration was able to dispose of the site again after a positive ruling.

At the end of 2021, the municipality confirmed that 18.9 million zloty will finally be allocated for initial restoration work. As you're reading this, it might already be possible to visit this amazing gem again!

67 Penitent Bridge

Where you end up if you just play with love…

🚊 Szewska 10 🚏 Wita Stwosza 🕐 Daily 10 – 19h, during summer season till 20h 🅿 Mostek Pokutnic w Katedrze św. Marii Magdaleny 🌐 katedramm.pl/mostek-pokutnic » Take in the book store smell at Tajne Komplety **87**!
💡 No elevator available!

One of the oldest buildings in Wrocław is the St. Mary Magdalene Church, originally built in 1342-1362. A church stood there as early as the eleventh century, but it was destroyed in 1241 during the Mongol invasion. Its successor, built on the same site between 1242 and 1248, did not have a long life either, as it was destroyed by a fire in 1342. And although it is said that history does not repeat itself, this is not entirely true in the case of the St. Mary Magdalene Church: although it survived the Second World War in relatively good condition, it caught fire and partially collapsed ten days after the city's surrender to the Red Army.

But it is not only the building itself that has historical significance for the city: In 1523, Johann Hess held the first Protestant mass in Wrocław there. Today, however, the imposing sacred Gothic building is less famous for its history rather than for a particular structural detail: the tiny footbridge that connects the two church towers 45 metres above the ground.

The name „Penitent Bridge" has its origins in an old legend. Once upon a time, there was a vain and lazy girl from Wrocław named Tekla, who had as little in mind with proper housekeeping as she did with marriage and starting a family. According to legend, the young lady preferred instead to turn men's heads and just have a good time for herself. Her father was not very enthusiastic about this and put a curse on her – he had her taken to the bridge where she had to stay for all eternity. You can find out how the story ended by climbing the 247 steps.

But the climb is worth it anyway, as it is one of the most beautiful viewing points in the city. Those who are unafraid of being trapped on the bridge forever should therefore make their way up and enjoy the great panorama view. And by the way, one of the famous dwarfs from Wrocław is hiding on the bridge as well…

68 Pergola and the Multimedia Fountain

F *Where light, water, and music shows meet wedding dresses*

🚆 Wystawowa 1 🚊 Hala Stulecia 🕐 During summer season, shows happen at every full hour between 10-22h 🇵🇱 Pergola we Wrocławiu / Wrocławska Fontanna Multimedialna 🌐 wroclawskafontanna.pl ⏩ Admire the Four Domes Pavilion 21

Just behind the Centennial Hall, you will come across Wrocław's so-called „multimedia fountain". If you're thinking of a small fountain with a few sound and light effects in an average park, the name may sound a bit pretentious to your ears. But actually, we are talking big here – it is not as tiny as it sounds!

With 800 individually controllable light sources, 300 water jets, and even three fire jets, it is the largest fountain of its kind in Poland and one of the largest in Europe. It opened in 2009 to mark the 20th anniversary of free elections in post-communist Poland. Every hour during the summer season, music of all kinds of styles is played there, accompanied by a monstrous water and light show. Although there are also shows with relaxing music, the people of Wrocław especially love the rock-and-pop and film music shows.

Another big plus: the shows are free and can be watched from the surrounding green spaces. If the sun gets too hot in the summer, you can simply move on to the pergola: a magnificent, shady colonnade with a planted roof that has a total of 750 columns along its 640-metre length. It leads around the multimedia fountain in a semicircle.

The creator of the pergola is a well-known name in the city's architectural history: Hans Poelzig, who also designed the Four Dome Pavilion. The beauty of the pergola is no secret in Wrocław, which is why numerous wedding photographers take their business there. In summer, there are so many bridal couples that you almost feel like you're at a public fashion show. If you're looking for the perfect wedding dress, you can get some inspiration there!

69 Polinka Cable Car

A cable car in the City of Bridges

🚩 Na Grobli 2 🚌 Plac Wróblewskiego (Southern end), Most Grunwaldzki (Northern end) 🕐 Mon–Fri 7–16h, Sat+Sun 10–19h 🚏 Polinka
🌐 pwr.edu.pl/polinka ❱❱ Get back to town via the Grunwaldzki Bridge **24**

Although Wrocław is known as the „City of Bridges" or the „Venice of the East" (and sometimes the "Venice of the North"), some people prefer to cross the Oder River by kayak or boat. But there is a more unconventional way: a cable car!

It is up to each person to assess whether this is needed despite the huge amount of bridges, but at least it serves a pragmatic purpose: Polinka connects two faculties of the Wrocław University of Science and Technology *(Politechnika Wrocławska)*. Can there be a more stylish way to commute from one building to another? Surely not!

Rumours say that Polinka was built as an antidote to one of the students' favourite excuses for being late to class – which was to supposedly getting stuck on the shuttle bus due to heavy traffic on the bridge. Well, even today during peak hours, you can see students lining up for around 200m to get to the other side via the Polinka cable car, so at best, that old excuse has been replaced by a new one…

The journey takes less than three minutes and is free for employees and students of the university. But the price for all other passengers is very moderate (the equivalent of less than one euro), especially since you are rewarded with fantastic views of the Oder River. Even though the cable car, which holds a maximum of 15 people, does not connect any tourist attractions, it isn't far from the Hydropolis science centre, which invites people to explore the subject of water interactively and is very popular with families. On the north side, the beach bar Forma Płynna – with its cosy beach chairs – awaits students who are working on their projects during the summer, and, of course, visitors who want to enjoy a great view of the two gondolas that float across the Oder every few minutes.

Also, Wrocław's second water tower can be seen from the gondola itself – the beautiful cube-like building dates back to 1871 and has also served as a theatre stage.

70 Polish Poster Gallery

Why the Terminator movie poster looks different in Poland

🚇 Świętego Mikołaja 54/55 🚌 Rynek 🕐 Tue–Fri 12–17h
🇵🇱 Galeria Plakatu 🌐 polishposter.com
» Head over to the Neon Side Gallery, a very special cemetery **53**

Posters and Poland: The two not only start with the same letters but are much more connected than you would think. During the communist era, most movie productions from the West were not screened as most were not compatible with the propaganda ideas of the regime at the time.

However, after extensive review by the Ministry of Censorship, which could easily last several years, some hand-picked films were released. Nevertheless, the challenge of producing film posters for the local market remained. Before the globalised film industry, there were no agencies that completed this task for all markets. Moreover, the government had little interest in letting go of its control over the content of posters.

Consequently, Polish artists were commissioned to design these film posters. However, the artists were not able to watch the movies before the design was completed. Thus, many posters were created based purely on the title and without any detailed knowledge of the plot. This alone would certainly be a challenge, but it was often compounded by the misleading translations of the titles. For example, *Terminator* was translated as „The Electronic Assassin" – and posters were designed based solely on this information. Looking at them today, smirks are guaranteed.

But the poster culture in Poland is not limited to movies only. One of the best-known Polish poster designers is Ryszard Kaja. His interpretations of important Polish cities are very popular. He miraculously managed to capture the character of each city as a poster. Many of Kaja's designs can be purchased in the poster gallery. Most of his work is available as postcards too – so not having enough wall space at home doesn't mean you can't at least take a small souvenir.

71 Pomiędzy Café

In between – the translation can be taken literally

- Stanisława Dubois 2   Dubois   Daily 9:30–18h, Sun until 15h
- Pomiędzy cafe & bistro   facebook.com/pomiedzy.cafe
- Pay attention to the mysterious hand on the way back to the old town **45**

Pomiędzy means something like „in-between" and the longer you think about it, the clearer it becomes that this name wasn't chosen at random.

First of all, the café is geographically located in the triangle between the historic Old Town, the alternative district of Nadodrze, and Słodowa Island (the only place in Wrocław where alcohol can legally be consumed in public). The menu offers plenty of dishes for small or large appetites, for early breakfasts and late dinners, and everything in between.

But the corner building in which Pomiędzy Café resides, a tenement house from pre-war times, remains true to the „in-between" slogan. Fortunately, the ornaments framing the window next to the entrance door survived the war intact. On the left is a poor tramp with torn clothes – his look and empty pockets reveal that he is not doing particularly well financially. On the right hangs his well-groomed counterpart – a finely dressed gentleman presenting his savings book with great pride – who is a customer of the bank that used to be located there. The social differences may not be as significant today as they were back then, but Pomiędzy is still – you guessed it – in between. This place is more than just a small independent corner café: it hosts changing art exhibitions that are always worth a visit.

Last but not least, the owner of the café, Anna Policka, deserves some special credit. Along with her mother, she is preparing to take the title of „Land of Smiles" from Thailand to Poland. The wonderful hospitality, the delicious food and good coffee, and the works of art are everything your heart and body need. The summer smoothies and the homemade banoffee cake can't be missed!

72 The Postmodernism of Wojciech Jarząbek
C,F

Solpol might be gone, but postmodernism still lives

Former Solpol plot: Świdnicka 21-23 Świdnicka
Kolorowa Plomba 1996: ul. Wybrzeże Stanisława Wyspiańskiego 36
Kliniki - Politechnika Wrocławska
All year round Witness the former wealth of ul. Ofiar Oświęcimskich **91**

After communism fell in Poland, architects were suddenly able to freely express and design what they wanted, and a new era of architecture was born – postmodernism. This period is often referred to as "unleashing all creativity blocked for so long". Architects mostly designed housing and churches before as imposed by the government, but they could now take on entirely new projects unheard of. One of them was Wrocław-born architect Wojciech Jarząbek. And this is how the story of the highly controversial Solpol building begins…

In 1992, Zygmunt Solorz-Żak, one of the wealthiest people in Poland, asked Jarząbek to design a shopping mall complex, but he was in a hurry – he wanted the building plans to be ready in 120 hours! This wasn't a problem for Jarząbek, who executed this mission under the deadline with his team. Towards the end, they were so exhausted that the cleaning lady of their office was said to have picked the colours of the building, as she was the only one who had slept and had enough mental energy to make the decision.

The outcome was truly unique and many people openly loved and hated Solpol equally. In recent years, numerous debates were had regarding if the building deserved monumental protection as the "birth" of the postmodernist style in Wrocław, or if should it be destroyed for something new. Well, Sopol was eventually demolished in 2022 – the capital of the new investments overruled its preservation.

But that's no reason to be sad, as there are still traces of Jarząbek's work and plenty of buildings from the postmodernist period in Wrocław to be explored. A striking example is "Kolorowa Plomba 1996" which can be admired at ul. Wybrzeże Stanisława Wyspiańskiego 36. It comes very close to the colours and awkwardness of the original and now-defunct Solpol building. You can decide for yourself if it's art or an eyesore.

73 Przedwojenna Bistro

Creating connections with cheap beer and popular Polish snacks

- Świętego Mikołaja 81 ● Rynek ● Daily, almost around the clock
- Przedwojenna ›› Spend some time at the historic Market Square **27**

A true institution of the city is the *Przedwojenna* (pre-war) Bistro. The journey back in time begins the moment you walk through the front door. The long-forgotten sounds through the crackling of a gramophone and the old black-and-white photographs on the walls emphasise the impression that you left the 21st century and are now in a 1930s setting. The atmosphere, especially later in the evening, is characterised by loud conversations and meeting new random bar acquaintances.

Visitors who come to Wrocław without any knowledge of Polish will encounter a new definition of the „revolving door effect" here. Hardly anyone leaves the pub late at night without a – more or less – good knowledge of Polish. Przedwojenna not only offers drinks at bargain prices, an important reason for its popularity with residents and visitors alike, but it is also an ideal place to get classic Polish cuisine. There are numerous decent quality bar snacks at affordable prices to accompany a cold drink, including *gzik* (boiled potatoes with cottage cheese or curd), *tatar* (raw and low-fat beef with egg yolk, often served with onions, mustard, and cucumber), *kiełbasa* (sausage) and *śledzik* (herring). The menu is on the wall – all the dishes are painted there, so you can easily communicate with your hands and feet if your level of Polish isn't there yet. Przedwojenna is a must for any night out.

Tip: If it already looks crowded, be sure to check the upstairs area, as some guests often don't make it up the stairs anymore. Conveniently, the bistro is directly opposite the St. Elizabeth Church, so you can continue to the confession early on Sunday morning without detours or the need to go home first.

74 Quarter of Four Denominations
A colourful mix of religion, art, and nightlife

🚏 Świętego Antoniego und Pawła Włodkowica 🚇 Rynek
🕐 All year round 🔴 Dzielnica Czterech Świątyń
» Don't miss the Museum of Games and Computers of the Past Era **44**

The Quarter of Four Denominations has many names. It is often called the „Neighbourhood of Mutual Respect" or the „Four Temples Neighbourhood." Most of the terms derive from the same idea: the proximity of four different religions whose followers have lived together for centuries. Only a few steps apart from each other, there is a Protestant, a Catholic, and an Orthodox church. And, of course, a synagogue is also an integral part of this multicultural neighbourhood.

Today's Orthodox church, formerly St. Barbara's Church, has a special feature: its clock ran about 15 minutes behind real time for several centuries. According to official information, this was not a malfunction but intentional. Why? Well, to not disturb residents when so many other bells were already ringing. Creative homemakers discovered that the gap between the ringing of the various city church bells and that of the Orthodox Church could be put to good use. They gave the clock the name „Klößeseiger" (dumpling clock) – the ringing of the bells of St. Barbara's Church was the signal to put Silesian dumplings into the water and then removed with the ringing of the town hall clock – perfectly cooked! In 2014, the clock was finally restored and has been running in sync with the others. Fortunately, smartphone timers were invented in the meantime; otherwise, there probably would be no more dumplings cooked to perfection today.

The entrance gate to the Four Denomination District is the Crystal Planet sculpture. Created by Ewa Rossano, the sculpture wears our planet as a dress, a symbol of community and cohesion. It is also a popular meeting place to start the nightlife. Although religion traditionally plays an important role here, the quarter is anything but holy – it is rather one of the most popular hotspots of Wrocław's party scene. Numerous pubs, bars, and clubs are waiting to be explored here.

For the morning after, a visit to the funky OTO Coffee Bar (ul. Świętego Antoniego 28), one of the best spots in Wrocław for top-quality coffee, is highly recommended.

🔎 In the pictures: The Crystal Planet sculpture, the OTO Coffee Bar, and the "dumpling clock" of St. Barbara's Church.

75 Railway Embankment (Nasyp)
A pub street underneath the railway tracks

C

🚌 Wojciecha Bogusławskiego 🚋 Arkady (Capitol) 🕐 All year round
Ⓟ Nasyp ⏩ Visit the Monument of the Anonymous Pedestrians 42

Normally, railway station bars and the surrounding streets have a rather dubious reputation, no matter what city they are in. It is therefore astonishing that there is a lively pub street only five minutes away from the main station in Wrocław – and it isn't dominated by the drug milieu. On the contrary, *Nasyp* (railway embankment) on ul. Wojciecha Bogusławskiego enjoys enormous popularity, especially among students. Of course, every other crowd is welcome there and it ends up being a great blend of people.

Those expecting a normal pub street will, however, be surprised, because it is a collection of small and cosy bars and restaurants. „Small and cosy" applies here in the literal sense of the word, as they usually have the dimensions of a standard double garage. The atmosphere is unique because each of the thirty or so pubs is run independently and has its own character.

That said, all the pubs have one thing in common: due to their location in the railway embankment, the railway tracks run directly above the pubs. This means that every few minutes a train rolls over the heads of the visitors. It's not just the expected background noise, but also the vibrations that overwhelm the body may take some time getting used to. But don't worry, after the fifth train and the second beer, you hardly notice them anymore...

The 67 brick vaults were built in 1905 and cover a length of about 600 metres. After being owned by the local railway company for a long time, the gradual transformation from small shops to today's colourful pub mile began in the 1990s. Its popularity also originates from the fact that it is located away from the larger tourist crowds around the market square. Consequently, the prices here are reasonable – good for travellers on a budget and great to meet real locals!

pociąg
12
75

WARSTEINER
3) LITOVEL DARK 13,-
4) CYDR DOBROŃSKI 8,-
5) TRUSKAWKOWY PORTER 12,-
6) REBEL IPA 10,-
7) KLASYCZNA PSZENICA 10,-
8) MOTHER OF DRAGONS 12,-
(DRAGON FRUIT SOUR ALE) 15,-
BIMBER 7,-
WHISKY OD 10,-
RUMY (WHITE/GOLD/DARK) OD 10,-
GIN OD 10,-
TEQUILA (SILVER/GOLD) 12,-
BRANDY 11,-
WINO (RED/WHITE) 10,-
MIÓD PITNY (100 ML) 12,-
ABSINTH 11,-
JAGERMEISTER 10,-
CYNAR 8,-
MALIBU 8,-
MARTINI (150 ML)
BAILEYS
KAHLUA
PALE ALE
STOUT

76 Renoma

The escalators were once its biggest attraction

🗺 C

📍 Świdnicka 40 🚇 Renoma 🕐 Mon–Fri 9–21h
🇵🇱 Renoma 🌐 renoma-wroclaw.pl » Visit the Nawa Sculpture **50**

Certainly not a hidden gem, but one of the most interesting „older modern" buildings in the city is the Renoma department store. The modernist design by Hermann Dernburg has a three-dimensional look due to the tapering floors and could also be reminiscent of a giant cake if the building were round and had a cherry on top.

Built over the course of eight months and opened in 1930, Renoma was an absolute novelty in many ways. Some might assume that the modern National Forum of Music and the Renoma department store were designed by the same architect at around the same time, although many decades separate these buildings.

When Renoma opened (founded as Wertheim-Kaufhaus), it added several superlatives to Wrocław. It was the largest department store in the city – three times the size of its closest competitor – and the largest steel framework structure in all of Europe. But the architects faced huge obstacles because, like the Centennial Hall, there was massive opposition to the building.

There had previously been an upper-class hotel on the site, which was bulldozed to the ground. This led to a large boycott of the new capitalist building. However, it turned out to be a very smart move that the first escalators in the entire region were installed there. Even the skeptics were too curious to see them and the department store quickly rehabilitated its image even among former critics.

The approximately 100 sculptures on the facade, all of them human heads, have a story to tell as well. They were meant to represent the inhabitants of Wrocław – the wife of one of the sculpture artists can also be found there.

Renoma has been a listed building since 1977 and was extensively renovated in 2005. Even though half of it is empty today and there isn't much of the original splendour left, at least on the inside, it is definitely worth paying a visit. Another significant renovation is ongoing in 2022 and we soon will find out who the new long-term tenants are going to be.

77 The Royal Palace (Wrocław City Museum)

A panopticon of more than 1000 years of history

- Kazimierza Wielkiego 35 Zamkowa Wed–Sun 11–17h
- Pałac Królewski we Wrocławiu muzeum.miejskie.wroclaw.pl
- See the National Forum of Music, just around the corner 49

Among the many beautiful buildings in Wrocław with a chequered history is the City Castle, also known as Royal Palace in Wrocław. The small residence was built in 1717-1719 by the order of Baron Heinrich Gottfried Spaetgen. After his death, when Silesia already belonged to Prussia, the castle was taken over by King Frederick II in 1750, who transformed it into a royal residence – although he never lived there. Each Prussian king who succeeded Frederick II naturally wanted to leave his mark, and so several extensions followed.

Carl Gotthard Langhans, the architect of the Brandenburg Gate in Berlin, also designed two wing buildings there during Frederick II's lifetime, which were demolished in the meantime. During the war, parts of the building burnt down, and there were extensive renovations in 2000-2004 thanks to large private donations. The baroque garden in particular offers great photo opportunities.

Today, the Royal Palace is home to the Wrocław City Museum. The permanent „1000 Years of Wrocław" exhibition tells the complete story of the city, including topics that were considered taboo in communist times, such as the German past. Wrocław has returned to its multicultural roots and this is particularly telling in the way the museum explains the city's history not only in Polish and English but even in German. Maciej Łagiewski, the museum director, has an interesting background and is closely connected to the history of Wrocław. For example, the museum contains exhibits from his father, who was forced into labour in Germany. Łagiewski himself was active in the Solidarność movement and not only experienced the political uprising firsthand but also helped to shape it. He was also the main person responsible for the restoration of the Old Jewish Cemetery. For his life's work, he received the Cultural Award of Silesia from the state of Lower Saxony and the German Federal Cross of Merit.

78 The Salt Market Square

Flowers at any time of day or night

🌐 C

- Plac Solny 🚋 Rynek 🕐 All year round 🇵🇱 Plac Solny
- Find the DIY Crucifix Kit **18**

Like its big sibling, the historic Market Square right next door, the Salt Market Square was probably delineated in 1242 after the Mongol invasion. As the name suggests, salt was traded there, especially the white gold from the famous Wieliczka salt mine near Kraków. In addition, honey, ropes, wax, tea, and goat meat attracted the inhabitants to the Salt Market Square a few centuries ago.

Its importance seems to have been quite significant, as it was paved as early as 1361, an exception at this time. According to tradition, in addition to traders and their customers, the Salt Market Square ring also served as a meeting place for „Venezianer" – ore and mineral seekers to whom magical properties were attributed, the ancestors of Harry Potter, so to speak.

Until 1815, the Salt Market Square was one of the city's most popular markets, then the traders had to make way for new rules. In 1827, it was renamed *Blücherplatz* in honour of the Prussian field marshal general, who also received a monument.

With its destruction in 1945, the square regained its historical name. Unfortunately, most of the square was destroyed during the war, therefore many of the buildings are replicas. The most beautiful is undoubtedly the Old Stock Exchange, built in 1822-1825 and based on a design by Carl Ferdinand Langhans, with house number 16 being a magnificent example of neoclassicism with an Italian character.

Today, the salt market itself is primarily a flower market that is open 365 days a year around the clock. So if you need to apologise late at night after a marital fight, you are guaranteed to find the right flowers here.

A lesser-known detail is that there is a bunker underneath the square with an area of 1000 square metres that can provide shelter for up to 300 people. And a little irony of history: even before Wrocław became a Polish city, this market was colloquially called the „Polish Market" because many of the local vendors were of Polish nationality.

79 Sand Bridge and Cathedral Bridge
Why criminals once appreciated Cathedral Bridge

 D,E

📍 Most Piaskowy (Sand Bridge), Świętej Jadwigi 1 (Cathedral Bridge)
🚊 Hala Targowa 🕒 All year round 🚏 Most Piaskowy (Sand Bridge), Most Tumski (Cathedral Bridge) ➤ Of course, explore more of Cathedral Island **10**

Marking the beginning of Wrocław's history are two nearby historic bridges to Cathedral Island. So it only seems logical that the miraculous multiplication of bridges in the city began from this location.

Most Piasek (Sand Bridge), which is almost 32 metres long and 12 metres wide, was first mentioned in 1149. At that time, bridge construction technology was still in its infancy, so it is no longer possible to walk across the original bridge. There is evidence of it collapsing during a procession in 1423, and in 1709 the bridge was destroyed again, this time by the ever-feared floods of the Oder River. Today's bright red structure was built in 1861 and is still the oldest surviving bridge in the city.

Most Tumski (Cathedral Bridge) was built in 1889 and is less than a five-minute walk from Sand Bridge. At 52 metres long just under seven metres wide, it is a pedestrian bridge – unlike Sand Bridge. It was built in the 12th century as a wooden bridge and apparently, the aforementioned procession of 1423 led to its collapse.

In 2019, the bridge faced a different kind of threat: love locks! Their weight put so much pressure on the bridge that all the love locks had to be removed during a renovation. Despite the newly installed prohibition sign, the first locks have already sprouted again. Why on earth somebody would connect love with locks?

In earlier times, however, it was mostly criminals who loved Cathedral Bridge. It marked the beginning of the jurisdiction of the Bishop of Wrocław. In practical terms that meant scoundrels who managed to cross the bridge between 1504 and 1810 could escape prosecution by the city authorities and would only be liable to the church.

Above you see Cathedral Bridge, at the bottom Sand Bridge.

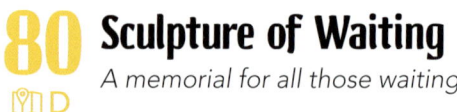Sculpture of Waiting
A memorial for all those waiting

- -

 Plac Powstańców Warszawy Urząd Wojewódzki
 All year round Rzeźba „Oczekiwanie"
 Walk along the Xawery Dunikowski Promenade 98

- -

According to studies, we spend a considerable part of our lives on an activity that is as simple as it is useless: waiting. We allegedly spend 156 hours per year waiting in front of a computer screen alone, and another 38 hours per year in traffic jams – to name just a few obvious categories. Public administration offices are also well known for long waiting times.

And to adequately „honour" this idle time, there is the Sculpture of Waiting in Wrocław's Słowacki Park: two large ceramic armchairs arranged side by side. One is free for visitors as a seat. It should be mentioned, however, that a young woman is waiting in the other armchair. She already seems slightly annoyed, because who likes to wait?

What is interesting here is that the viewer becomes part of the artwork. A visit should be a priority, after all, the young lady just wants to be relieved from waiting.

The sculpture was created in 1979 by two local artists: Anna Malicka-Zamorska and Ryszard Zamorski. Unfortunately, they had to wait no less than four decades to find themselves mentioned in this guidebook.

There is, of course, an alternative interpretation to this sculpture, as there is to almost every sculpture in Wrocław. It is expressed in the mocking epithet: „Monument to the Perfect Man" – a designation that undoubtedly refers to the empty space next to the lady. Also, it's just a coincidence that the armchairs bear a certain resemblance to the throne from the TV series *Game of Thrones*.

81 Słodowa Island

Balmy summer nights on the city's most popular island

🚇 Wyspa Słodowa 🚌 Dubois 🕐 All year round 📍 Wyspa Słodowa
» Explore the Quarter of Four Denominations 74

When the sun slowly fights its way through the grey clouds in spring and casts its first rays on Wrocław, a special kind of spectacle begins. That's when the doors of the student accommodations open, and everyone rushes to the well-known supermarket chains. Why? To stock up on beer and snacks, of course; and then to welcome spring together with friends on Słodowa Island. This might all sound a bit exaggerated, but Słodowa (with the ugly name „Vorderbleiche" in German times) is the most popular island in the city.

But Słodowa Island isn't just for the young. On sunny days, people of all ages and social classes make the pilgrimage to the island to celebrate together. After all, alcohol can legally be consumed here in public, an act that is normally punishable by huge fines. Picnics are prepared, board games are unpacked, a few musicians play along on their guitars, and young, physically fit people carefully balance between trees on the slackline. The island is always busy in summer, even late at night.

Thanks to its location, the island offers a dreamlike view of Wrocław University, one of the longest baroque facades in the world. The illuminated surrounding buildings create a magical atmosphere.

This is rounded off by several floating pubs that offer the best beer garden atmosphere and serve delicious cocktails, Polish beers, and snacks. The most recent addition is the rooftop bar on the terrace of the modernist Concordia building with the largest planted green wall in Poland. The place has quickly established itself in the upscale party scene and offers magnificent views of the area as well, and not only during sunsets!

💡 This is the roof terrace of the Concordia Design Building.

82 The Square of John Paul II

A journey into the culture of underground passages

🚇 Plac Jana Pawła II 🚋 Plac Jana Pawła II 🕐 All year round 🅿 Plac Jana Pawła II ⏩ Have you already seen the Train to Heaven? **90**

Many Wrocław residents associate the square of John Paul II first and foremost with the daily traffic chaos that takes place at this busy intersection at the entrance to the city. The former glory of the former King's Square *(Königsplatz)*, one of the largest and most attractive squares in the entire city, has long since faded.

As early as 1820, the now-demolished Nikolai gate was generally considered the most beautiful entrance to the city. Some of its remains can still be found today at the St. Joseph Church. But another development is fairly exciting: the square was simply moved underground in 1984 to make more space for cars. This created a pedestrian subway typical of the Soviet era with its very own charm – a rather dreary underground world with many small shops such as kiosks, clothing shops, cafés, shops full of cheap Chinese products, bakeries, or an Irish Pub with pool tables. Flying merchants sell their home-picked berries and mushrooms here on the street. Tourists wearing Jack Wolfskin functional clothing will be easily spotted and identified as non-local visitors – but why not leave your comfort zone and try something unusual?

From the pizzeria, which is present on the stairs leading back to the light, the view falls on the former city moat, of which a small pond is still left there. It serves as the foreground for one of the latest investment projects – the transition of a huge former German hospital complex into apartments and a new old town boulevard.

Back at the street level in daylight, the smell of petrol and diesel wafts around you. But coincidentally, one of the most popular spots for wedding pictures can be found: the Fountain of Flight and Victory! This is probably due more to its proximity to the civil registry office than to the sculpture itself, which was created in 1905 by Ernst Seger and Bernhard Sehring. It shows the fight between a well-built man and a lion.

Not far from there, the Quorum Tower is currently being built, another massive skyscraper with lots of office and residential space. It will be interesting to see how the underground passage and the surrounding area will change in the coming years.

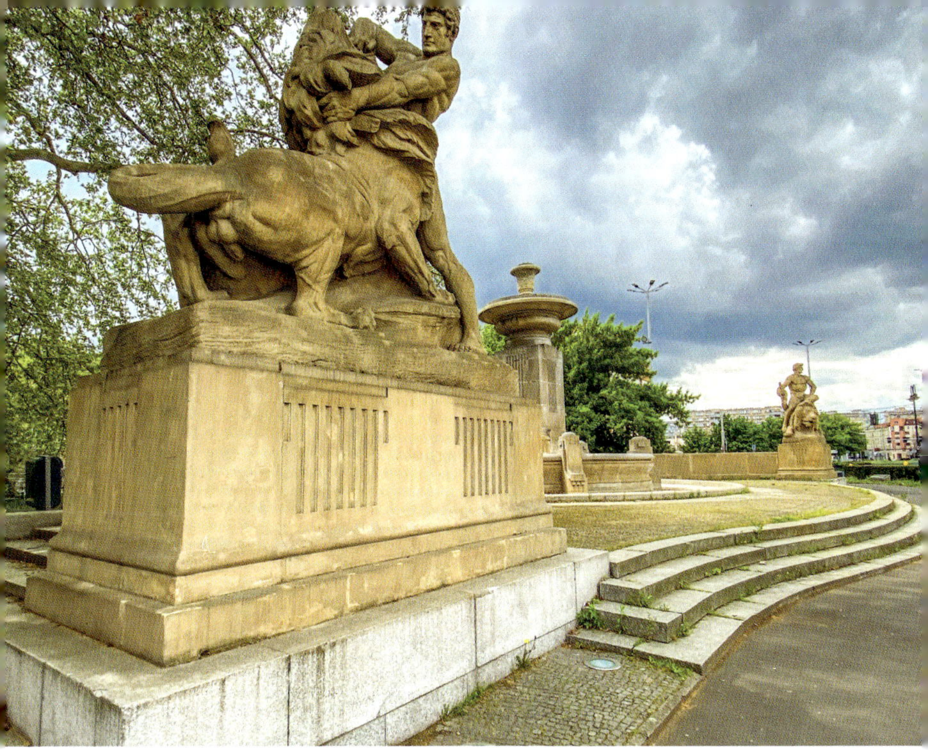

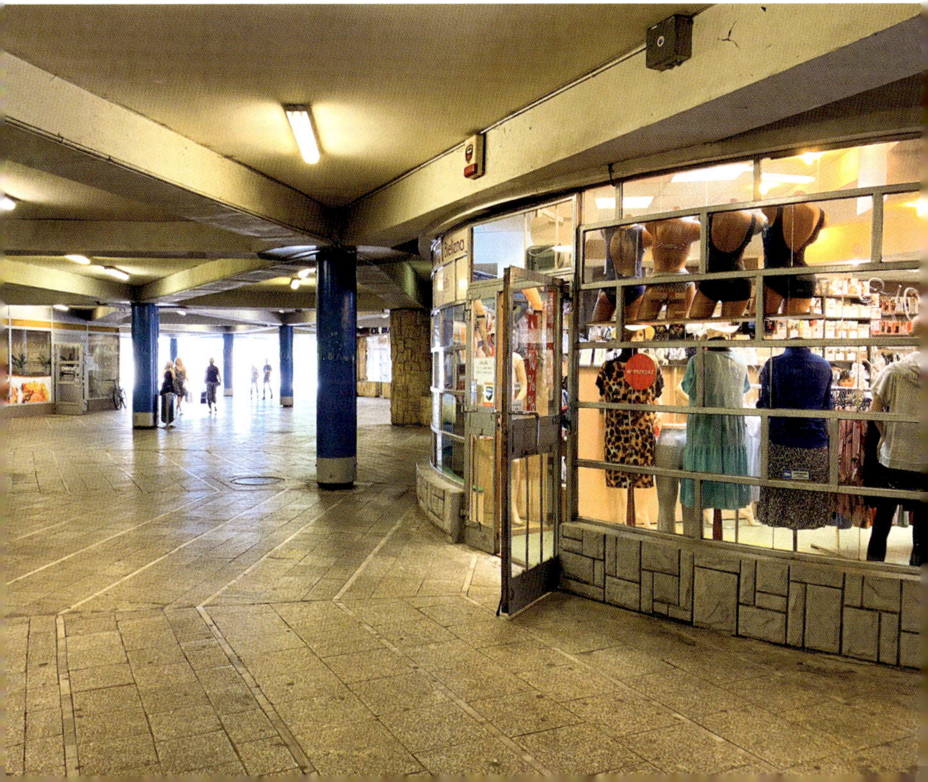

83 Stare Jatki

The miraculous transformation of mounds of meat into mounds of art

🍴 Jatki 20 🚇 Uniwersytet Wrocławski 🕐 All year round 🇵🇱 Stare Jatki
» Check out the giant Concrete Chair **22**

One of the questions frequently asked by visitors to Wrocław is where the best place is to buy some artworks made by real local artists. The answer: at *Stare Jatki* (Old Butchers). But don't worry, there hasn't been any real meat there for a long time.

The medieval street first saw the light of day around the 13th century. The street originally consisted of 48 small wooden stalls, 24 on each side of the street. In the 14th century, these were replaced by small stone houses. Although the stalls were only rented out to the butchers by the city, they considered them as their property and lived there themselves, even without official permission. However, the meat lobby was strong enough even back then to win some related conflicts, and in the end, the city not only approved the conversion of the wooden shacks into residential apartments but even allowed them to be extended by height. The butchers also enjoyed several other privileges, including so-called „mileage rights" – the equivalent to a monopoly, because no one was allowed to pursue this profession within a radius of about seven kilometres around the city without a licence.

Meat was processed and sold there up into the 19th century. Today, however, the 30-square-metre plots are mostly used to sell art. In addition to more traditional souvenir shops, there are numerous artist studios that provide an exciting insight into the craftsmanship of the region. The upper floors are still used as living spaces.

The most popular picture spot on Stare Jatki is waiting at the entrance. It is not the butcher's dwarf, which, of course, cannot be missed either, but the „Monument to the Slaughtered Animals" – a 1997 creation by artist Piotr Wieczorek. It admonishes from the perspective of our four-legged friends – the interpretation is, of course, up to everyone. The small commemoration sign reads: "In honour of the slaughtered animals" and it's signed by „The consumers".

84 Świebodzki Railway Station
From a regional train station to the place of culture

C

📍 Plac Orląt Lwowskich 20b 🚊 Plac Orląt Lwowskich
🕐 Flea Market during summer season every Sunday from 6–15h,
the street food hall Mon–Wed 12–0h, Thu 12–2h, Fri+Sat 12–4h, Sun 17–0h
🚇 Świebodzki 🌐 halaswiebodzki.pl ➡ Don't skip the underground vibes at the Square of John Paul II **82**

Completed in 1842, the Świebodzki Railway Station is the oldest preserved railway station in the city, even though the impressive neo-classical style facade was only built between 1868 and 1874. In German times it was called „Freiburger Bahnhof".

In the early years, however, there was not a wide range of connections – the trains only headed for the small town of Freiburg in Silesia, 58 km away, not to be confused with the better-known Freiburg im Breisgau.

The "turntable" is an interesting detail, where the trains could be turned around in the opposite direction and then travel back. However, you won't find any trains there anymore, as operations were discontinued in 1991. Today, the building is home to a music school, a theatre, and a club, as well as the exciting Museum of Games and Computers of the Past Era, and a board game café.

The main attraction is undoubtedly the weekly flea market, which takes place every Sunday from six in the morning. Just like the flea market at the Old Mill, Polish families come together early in the morning to hunt for bargains, with a strong focus on clothing at this location, although there are also goods and groceries such as fruit and vegetables. And the prices are still below average.

After the official part of the flea market concludes, there is more: on the railway tracks, private individuals then sell all kinds of things more or less professionally directly from the boots of their cars…

Since 2020, the railway station has also gained a newly designed street food hall – if you like, you can eat your Asian curry together with a cool drink right next to the train tracks.

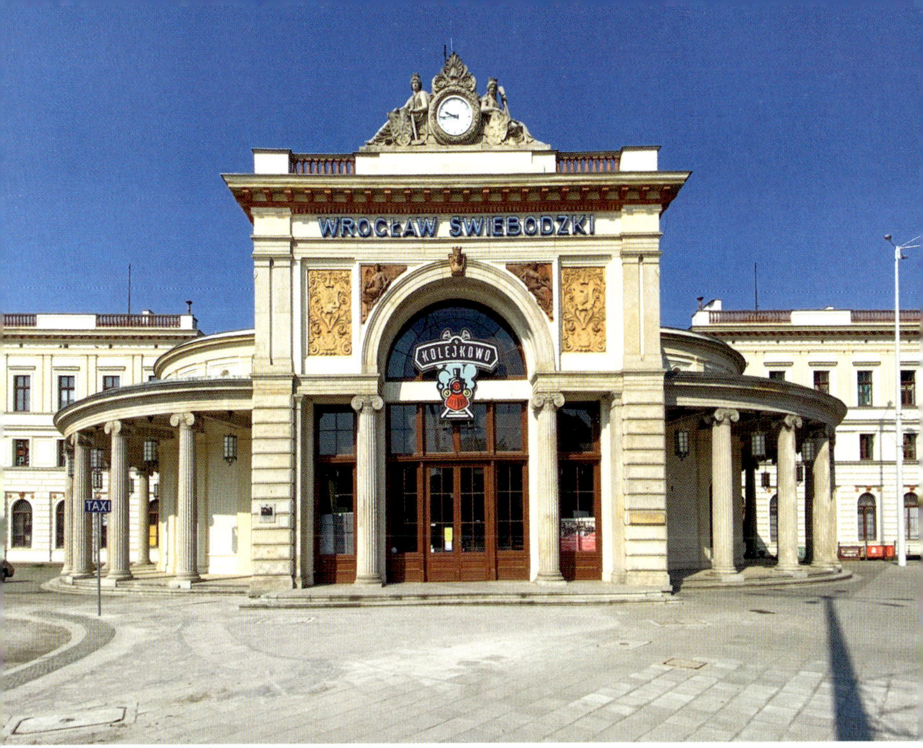
WROCŁAW ŚWIEBODZKI
KOLEJKOWO
TAXI

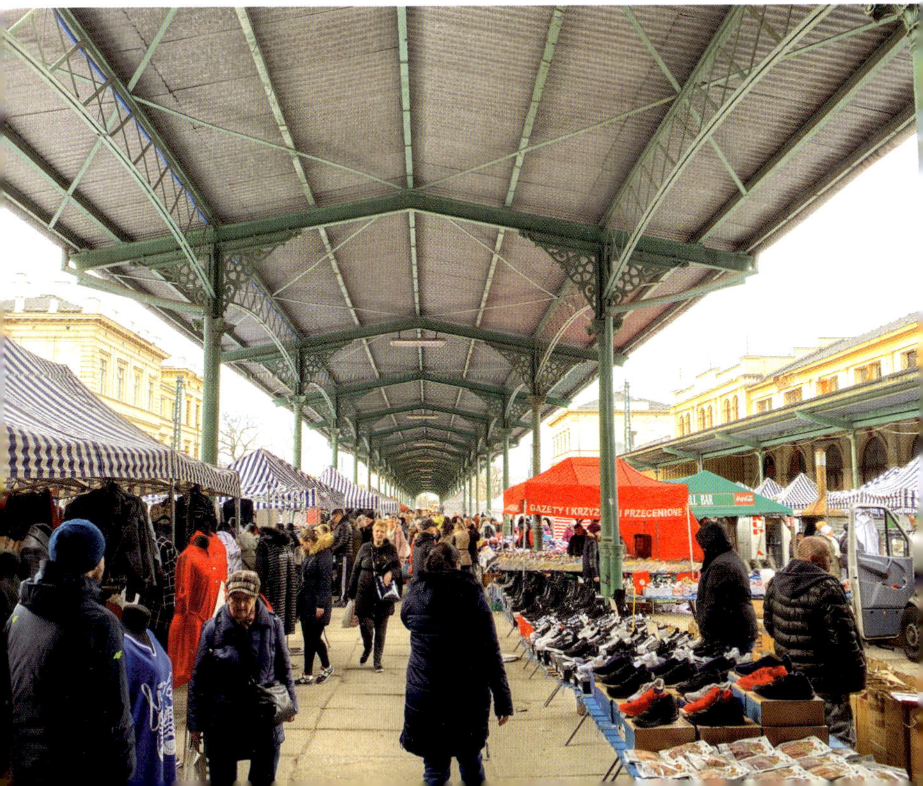

85 Szczytnicki Park and the Japanese Garden

The city's largest park offers plenty of shade and tranquillity

🚏 Adama Mickiewicza 1 🚊 Park Szczytnicki 🕐 April to October, 9–19h
📍 Park Szczytnicki, Ogród Japoński 🌐 ogrod-japonski.wroclaw.pl
»» Visit Mała Czarna **35**

Believe it or not, Wrocław, according to some sources, is the greenest city in Poland. At least statistically speaking, each inhabitant has 25 square metres of park space to themselves. One of the most beautiful parks was formerly known as Scheitniger Park *(Park Szczytnicki)* and was laid out in 1785. With a total area of more than 100 hectares, it is now the most extensive of its kind and can proudly bear the title of „Wrocław's largest park".

Thanks to its dimensions, every visitor is guaranteed to find a nice shady or sunny spot there, surrounded only by the chirping of birds. Thus, the park represents a total oasis of tranquillity and is the ideal place to read a book, soak up some sun, or simply relax a little in summer. The northern part is strongly reminiscent of an urban forest, especially towards the northeast, where the park ends at Mała Czarna (an amazing, but well-hidden café in the city) in the Olympic area.

It is also interesting to note that one of the few monuments with a connection to the German past can be found there. Dedicated to Friedrich Schiller, the monument was destroyed after the war as part of the Polonization process but rebuilt on the same site in 1995 as a sign of reconciliation on the 190th anniversary of his death.

The Japanese Garden, located in the southern part, was initially laid out only for the Centennial Exhibition of 1909-1912. It wasn't until 1995 that the garden was lavishly reconstructed. Unfortunately, the joy was short-lived, as only two years later, 70 percent of the area was destroyed by the Millennium Flood, and reconstruction was necessary once again.

Incidentally, the name of the park, *Hakkoen* (white and red garden), alludes to the same-coloured flags of Poland and Japan. The Centennial Hall with the pergola and the colourful multimedia fountain are in the immediate vicinity and can't be missed.

◉ On top you see the Japanese Garden, at the bottom Szczytnicki Park.

86 Szklarnia

Cocktails in a hipster greenhouse

📍 C

- Ofiar Oświęcimskich 19 🚇 Świdnicka 🕐 Mon–Thu 14–1h, Fri+Sat 14–4h, Sun 14–0h 🍷 Szklarnia 🌐 szklarniawroclaw.business.site
- Don't miss out on Browar Stu Mostów for more beer **6**

When meeting younger tourists in Wrocław who traveled by train from surrounding cities and looking to dive into the Polish nightlife, it's easy to recommend *Szklarnia* (greenhouse). The name says it all, as the ambience is like a large and cosy conservatory, especially during the day when the natural light floods into the bar through the huge windows.

On the walls, you'll find bicycles and lots of hanging green plants, which together with the radiant lighting create an alternative hipster feeling in the later evening hours. The gardeners from Szklarnia have also gone wild in the courtyard and created a beautiful environment for the guests. There may not be too many traditional beer gardens in Wrocław, but that isn't a problem at all, as the beach bars and the many hidden and colourful courtyards are more than adequate substitutes.

It's not just the décor that makes this particular greenhouse a popular stop in Wrocław's nightlife. The cocktails are put together with great attention to detail. When the cocktail seems to be ready at the bar, that's when the final touches are added – a little mint here and a few rose petals there. The drink is only served in perfection – shame on anyone who takes it too early!

Szklarnia is ideal for larger groups and especially birthday parties because the space is huge and there are separate areas for celebrations. Those who still can't find a seat during a spontaneous late-night visit need not despair – there are several legendary pubs in the immediate surroundings, like the craft beer bar Kontynuacja, the place where craft beer culture was born in Wrocław.

87 Tajne Komplety

A reminder of the times when people had to hide

 Przejście Garncarskie 2 Wita Stwosza Daily 12–19h, Sun until 17h Café Księgarnia Tajne Komplety tajnekomplety.pl
 Check out the concert schedule from Vertigo Jazz Club **93**

Poland's history unfortunately has various periods of oppression. During those times, it was not always possible to communicate openly in Polish or to familiarise yourself with the culture of your nation. But pragmatically, as Poles are, they looked for creative solutions. They set up secret educational centres called *Tajne Komplety* where they defied the oppressors and passed on knowledge about Poland's history, language, and culture to the younger generations.

The bookshop Tajne Komplety was named after these institutions. Maybe it's on purpose or just a coincidence, but the shop is slightly hidden and can easily be overlooked. Yet it is right in the middle of the action on the Market Square, or rather, inside the Market Square. Three small alleys run through the buildings in the middle of the square, and the shop is located in one of them.

Tajne Komplety is by no means a conventional bookshop, but rather a hybrid of a bookshop, café, cultural centre, and trendy meeting place. Live in a small space by yourself? There's no need to be sad knowing that this cosy oasis with the most comfortable upholstered furniture in town is close by. Outside of the chance to play a round of chess, Tajne Komplety offers regular readings, film screenings, concerts, and other events that make this café a meeting place that is just as popular with the intellectual scene as it is with „normal" visitors of Wrocław.

There are probably more than just a few people who would be willing to give up their flat in exchange for a room in this bookshop. Guests in Wrocław will not only discover the intense smell of books and good coffee, but also numerous nice souvenirs to share with those at home, including postcards, posters, and regional literature in various languages.

The Traces of History in Nadodrze
When the past knocks at your door

- Paulińska Paulińska All year round „Poniemieckie" napisy
- https://www.wroclawguide.com/en/german-traces-wroclaw-tour
- Try pierogi from Bar Pierożek 2

After the end of the war in 1945, Wrocław was placed under the Polish administration. This marked the beginning of the transformation process, and the formerly German city became part of Poland pretty much overnight.

Along with this, all the German traces were removed – monuments, gravestones, and street and shop names. With great care, house fronts were repainted with fresh paint. Ornaments in German were also made unrecognisable with a hammer and sickle. Over the decades, however, a combination of erosion from weather, a lack of maintenance, and the limited lifespan of the paints used has caused the facades to slowly reveal themselves again. Suddenly, the old German inscriptions stood out in many places. Between Polish nail salons and hairdressers, a traditional German pub *(Gastwirtschaft)* or a workshop for modern footwear *(Werkstatt für moderne Fußbekleidung)* appears.

In many parts of Wrocław, you can find such traces of the German past, but there is quite an accumulation of these spots in the Nadodrze district, mostly due to the former German tenement houses that survived the war relatively unscathed. Dealing with the evidence of the past can sometimes be controversial today. As many of the buildings concerned are in poor condition structurally and are being lavishly restored – often with the help of European Union funds – some of the owners have decided to erase the German traces once again. On the other hand, others have honoured the past and taken it with them into the future – they kept the German inscriptions and even repainted them.

A comprehensive documentation of all the traces has recently been carried out as part of the Looking at Breslau under the Plaster *(Spod tynku patrzy Breslau)* initiative. The locations of all the visible traces of history were identified and photographs were collected. A corresponding thematic city map is available online and offline.

> You can find these traces everywhere in the city if you pay close attention.

89 Traditional Pączki Pastry Shops
No, pączki are not donuts! Or maybe they are?

C

Ruska 10 | Rynek | Mon–Fri 7:30–19:30h, Sat 10–18h, Sun 13–18h
Cukiernia Łomżanka | Find healthier food at Wilk Syty **95**

One of Poland's most popular desserts is the so-called „pączki". But what is it exactly? If you ask a Pole whether they are donuts, you are usually met with a critical and very suspicious look. Of course not, they are just pączki.

Nevertheless, as with donuts, they are yeast pastries fried in fat. Typical fillings are jam or Nutella, but actually, anything sweet can be put into a pączki. The difference between a donut and a pączek is easy to spot – the pączek lacks the hole in the middle. But what distinguishes it from a real donut in terms of taste? It's hard to explain, so it's best to ask a Pole.

As with so many things here, religious traditions play a role. Traditionally, pączki are eaten in huge quantities on *Tłusty Czwartek* (Fat Thursday) – the Thursday before Ash Wednesday. This day used to be the last chance before the period of fasting to quickly use up any leftover sugar and fruit, which were forbidden and would therefore have gone to waste.

The tradition was so popular that Polish emigrants exported it to the USA. And the demand for the pastry was so great that Shrove Tuesday also became a designated Pączki Day. Did this replace Fat Thursday? Of course not, today people simply celebrate on both days and eat twice as many pączki.

One of the most traditional places to enjoy this treat is Cukiernia Łomżanka. This is probably the oldest confectionery in Wrocław, run by the third generation of the family, and is more or less the starting point of the pączki cult in Wrocław. It was founded in Łomża in 1935 and then moved to Wrocław after the war in 1953.

A little further out on one of the city's most beautiful streets, at ul. Curie-Skłodowskiej 51, is Pod Trumienką, which is also considered to be one of the best traditional pączki sources in town.

90 The Train to Heaven
The largest urban sculpture in Poland

🗺 A

📍 Plac Strzegomski 🚇 Plac Strzegomski (Muzeum Współczesne)
🕐 All year round 🇵🇱 Rzeźba „Pociąg do nieba" we Wrocławiu
» Obviously go to the Bunker Roof Terrace for another perspective of this sculpture 7

Wrocław has always been a city of superlatives – and still is today. The world's largest organ once stood here, and Wrocław still has, among other things, what was once the world's largest reinforced concrete building (Centennial Hall), Poland's longest suspension bridge, and one of the oldest restaurants in Europe.

So it's hardly surprising that Poland's largest urban sculpture was unveiled in Wrocław in 2010. Andrzej Jarodzki's massive creation is a TY2-1035 steam locomotive from 1944, which in its original state weighs 74 tonnes and has a length of around 30 metres – the highlight, however, is that the train stands on a track that points towards the sky.

Depending on the source, the weight of the sculpture is between 80 and 90 tonnes, and it's difficult to confirm this by simply lifting it, but feel free to give it a try. The dimensions of the object and its imposing nature alone literally overwhelm you. In this context, the artist speaks of dreams and desires that are expressed in the sculpture, as well as transcending the space of possibility.

However, with „transcending the space of possibility" he probably didn't mean to ask the people of Wrocław to literally climb up the train – something that does happen every now and then. The regional newspaper Gazeta Wrocławska couldn't resist the wordplay in the headline „Another man boarded the train to heaven"...

Even if a short trip to Wrocław doesn't leave time for a train ride to heaven, it should at least be noted that the sculpture stands directly on the route between the airport and the city centre. Almost all buses and taxis pass by there, so it's worth leaving your smartphone in your pocket and looking around – the train is hard to miss.

91 ul. Ofiar Oświęcimskich
The former street of the rich and beautiful

🗺 C

- Ofiar Oświęcimskich 🚊 Świdnicka 🕐 All year round
- 🇵🇱 Ofiar Oświęcimskich ⏩ Explore the Salt Market Square and its flower market **78**

There are many historical monuments on ul. Ofiar Oświęcimskich, but what's even more interesting were the personalities who lived on what was once one of the city's wealthiest streets. Ostentation, wealth, and excess: a good example of this is Heinrich Rybisch, a royal councillor under Emperor Ferdinand I and a resident of this street.

Rybisch was in charge of the demolition of a beautiful 12th-century abbey, the stones of which were subsequently „recycled" among other things for the construction of his own magnificent house at number 1. During his lifetime (1485-1544) this was only a persistent rumour, but it was confirmed posthumously by archaeologists. The portal of the house is still preserved. It was restored in 1997 and only provides a hint of how splendid and lavish the interior decoration may have been. Rybisch's tomb, also opulent of course, can still be seen in the St. Elizabeth Church today.

At number 15, on the other hand, is the former beerhouse of Conrad Kissling, which relocated to what was then Junkernstraße in 1851. Kissling opened the beerhouse at the age of 25 and was one of the best-known names in the local brewing scene. The inscription was only half-heartedly obscured after the war, so his name is still recognisable today. The previous Junkernstraße house number 9 is still engraved, but today's actual house number is 15.

The old traditions are now being continued in the adjacent building – number 17 – where the previously mentioned craft beer pub Kontynuacja stands. The name, translated as „continuation," is an allusion to Kissling. The famous architect Hans Poelzig, responsible for the construction of the Four Dome Pavilion, once lived here also.

Another milestone in the history of the street is the founding of Poland's first computer company (ZETO) in 1964. The building stands out with its modern architecture, which forms quite a striking contrast in comparison to the old magnificent houses.

9

CONRAD KISCHNE

MUZEUM

92 The University and the Aula Leopoldina
D
One of the longest baroque facades in the world

Plac Uniwersytecki 1 Uniwersytet Wrocławski Daily 10–16h (October to April), Mon–Fri 10–17h and Sat–Sun 10–18h (May to September) Uniwersytet Wrocławski, Aula Leopoldina muzeum.uni.wroc.pl Enjoy the perspective from Słodowa Island 81

As early as 1409, the city council is said to have voted in favour of founding a university, but this request was not formally confirmed until 1505 by the Bohemian King Vladislav II. Thanks to generous support from Emperor Leopold I, the university was finally founded in 1702 with the faculties of philosophy and theology. It just took 200 years to get there.

As it turned out, the entire history of the university's construction was marked by considerable obstacles. Not only did wars delay the start of construction, but also natural forces such as floods, as well as political power struggles. The west wing was completed in 1736 and the east wing four years later. Then the irony of history struck: immediately after the building was completed, the First Silesian War (1740-1742) began, and Silesia fell to the Prussians. In 1741, the building was transformed into a hospital, and it wasn't until 1763 that normal university operations could resume.

Over the years, further renovations took place, and surprisingly, despite all the wars, the baroque masterpiece still stands today. At 171 metres in length, the impressive baroque facade is one of the longest in the world. An interesting detail is the richly decorated door with the double-headed eagle, the symbol of the Habsburg monarchy. It bears the initials of the founder Leopold I – the L and the I together form a U, which stands for „Universitas".

It's also worth seeing the Mathematical Tower, a 40-metre-high sightseeing point that originally served as an observation point for astrophysicists. Today it is part of the university museum and offers impressive panoramic views of the city centre as well as the Oder River, with some of its islands on the other side. On top of the tower is a meridian line drawn in 1791 to accurately measure the noon hour – the only one of its kind in Poland.

The statues in the corners of the tower represent the four faculties: Theology, Philosophy, Law, and Medicine. Originally, three identical towers were planned, but due to turbulent circumstances during construction, only one was realised.

No less impressive is the Aula Leopoldina, a hall that is still used today for important ceremonies. The extensive baroque details in it have survived various wars and now delight architecture lovers from all over the world.

Even modern crime uses the university as a setting: in 1997, eight oil paintings were stolen with the thieves escaping through a window. For a long time, the paintings remained missing until one of the people involved struck a deal with law enforcement authorities. In exchange for two paintings, he was granted immunity from prosecution. Unfortunately, this did him little good, because a short time later he was found murdered under mysterious circumstances.

The university is, in a sense, the heart of Wrocław – and a total of around 140,000 students that make up all of the city's universities ensure a young and fun-loving flair almost everywhere.

93 Vertigo Jazz Club
Jazz – the favourite music of Wrocław

🗺 D

- 📍 Oławska 13 🚋 Oławska 🕐 Sun–Thu 18–0h, Fri+Sat 18–2h
- Vertigo Jazz Club 🌐 vertigojazz.pl
- » Have a glass of wine after the concert at Cocofli **16**

Jazz and *Wrocław* are often mentioned in the same sentence. Throughout the city centre, you can find street musicians who are slowly earning their place in the city's music scene. The standards are very high and the biggest destination – at least for jazz musicians – is without question the Vertigo Jazz Club.

Even with around 200 seats, the best jazz club in town has an intimate and cosy atmosphere. Top-class musicians regularly perform there and offer audiences fantastic live experiences.

There can often be surprises, like when an enthusiastic audience finds mysterious envelopes under their tables that actively involve them in the concert – those who are lucky received a spontaneous invitation to the stage.

Once a year, the Vertigo team organises a very special event: the Vertigo Summer Jazz Festival. Concerts are usually held daily from the beginning to the end of July at selected and unusual locations throughout the city, such as beach bars or on the roof terrace of the Monopol Hotel. How about a concert in the urban-industrial ambience of a tram depot? No problem – anything is possible.

It's not just jazz fans who get their money's worth there, but fans of all similar genres like swing and blues, as well as pop, soul, and funk. The events where modern interpretation of film music is presented are certainly exciting. There is even a regular Quentin Tarantino evening – an absolute hidden gem. Ticket prices are very affordable at 30-40 zloty, and on some evenings admission is even free.

94 The Water Tower

Probably the most impressive water tower in the world

A

🚆 Sudecka 125A 🚌 Sudecka 🕐 All year round, but currently not open to the public ⬤ Wieża Ciśnień ⏩ Visit the Old Jewish Cemetery 60

The 63-metre-high water tower in the south of Wrocław has been used for many purposes since being built in 1905. It was based on a design by Karl Klimm, a city building official who left his signature on many places around Wrocław, such as the Technical University and the Zwierzyniecki Bridge. The influences of Art Nouveau can be seen in the sculptures, while the tower is a mixture of Neo-Gothic and Neo-Romantic styles. It is often cited as a characteristic example of late eclecticism. Also, very untypical for the time, it was built with an electric elevator.

Originally planned as just a water tower, it had a dual function right from the start. At a height of 42 metres, there is a platform with a fantastic view of the Ślęża Mountain which is around 30 km away. In clear weather, the view even reaches as far as the Sudeten Mountains with Śnieżka as its highest point (1.603 m). In the early 20th century, when the view was particularly clear, a red flag would be raised.

During the war, it seemed only logical to set up a fire control post and a combat observation point there. Fortunately, the tower withstood the bombardment of the immediate surroundings. Until the 1980s, it served as a water tower again for the southern parts of Wrocław. A private investor acquired the historic building from the city in 1995 and a costly renovation followed. After its completion, a restaurant was opened in the tower. Unfortunately, it is currently closed to the public and access is not possible.

In 2020, the property was offered on the real estate market for just under five million euros, and its future is still unclear as of 2023. Whatever the future holds, it is an absolute gem and one of the most impressive water towers in the world!

95 Wilk Syty

Wrocław's paradise for vegans and vegetarians

Trzebnicka 3 ● Paulińska ● Daily 12–20h ● Wilk Syty
facebook.com/WilkSytyWroclaw/ ❱❱ The Heart of Nadodrze is just around the corner, make sure to visit it **25**

Once upon a time…a group of tourists were having breakfast in one of Wrocław's cafés and talked about how difficult it was to find good vegetarian restaurants in the city. As a local, you can only smile at the ignorance, because Wrocław is a paradise for fans of vegan and vegetarian cuisine.

If you don't believe it, you'll find a real hidden gem at *Wilk Syty* (Full Wolf), and indeed: after the special culinary journey that guests take, they are guaranteed to return home or to the nightlife highly satisfied. All former hungry wolves will have turned into full ones.

The menu's many seasonal dishes change weekly, and colourful surprises are guaranteed on the plate! If you're in the mood for successful experiments, this is the place to be. In autumn, for example, you'll be tempted by the fried mushrooms, delicately coated in sesame salt, served with carrot puree in miso sauce, caramelised pears, limes, and the whole dish garnished with hazelnuts.

The lovingly designed interior exudes cosiness and encourages even full wolves to eat a piece of cake afterward. And not only vegans and vegetarians will find Wilk Syty to be one of the best addresses for a special meal. Rumour has it that one or two meat lovers have been „converted" here - the food is so good that you simply don't miss meat at all. Those who still believe that healthy meals consist exclusively of lettuce leaves will be amazed – so why not try something new?

Finally, it should be mentioned that Wilk Syty is far from being the only exceptional restaurant for vegans. Bez Lukru, somewhat hidden in a side street off the market square (ul. Igielna 14), is also a popular meeting place for the local vegan foodie scene.

96 Wrocław Christmas Market

A great festival with visitors from all over the world

🗺 C

- 📍 Rynek 🚊 Wita Stwosza 🕐 Mid-November till 31 December
- 🇵🇱 Jarmark Bożonarodzeniowy
- 🌐 wroclawguide.com/en/the-christmas-market-in-wroclaw/
- ⏩ Find some peace and silence at the Ossolineum Garden **63**

Every year, towards the end of November, it's that time again: one of the most beautiful Christmas markets in Europe opens (don't take our word for it, even *Huffington Post* named the Wrocław Christmas Market as one of the twelve best in Europe). The smell of cinnamon, oranges, gingerbread, and mulled wine envelops the entire Wrocław Market Square and its surrounding area while the colourful lights fight the darkness and the low temperatures of winter.

Numerous stalls with handmade crafts, regional cuisines, and a vast selection of different mulled wine flavours, along with stages full of exciting shows, await the many visitors. But it is not only Germans and Ukrainians who make up the most significant part of the foreign visitors who make the pilgrimage to experience the unique atmosphere. The Wrocław Christmas Market is also highly popular within Poland and a popular destination for locals from all across the country.

Oscypek cheese is worth trying. It's a specialty from the Tatra region that is hard to find outside Poland. This elastic, smoked cheese made from sheep's milk has been traditionally produced for centuries. Lightly grilled and served with cranberries, Poles appreciate it as a tasty little snack.

A minor (or major, depending on your perspective) incident from 2019 reflects the market's popularity. Every year, the mulled wine cups are made in the shape of shoes and painted with Christmas motifs along with the current year. Despite the high deposit, the mugs quickly became popular collector's items, and after just a few days, there were none left. Scandalously, this meant that visitors had to drink with 2017 mugs. More interestingly, a huge black market developed for the 2019 mugs, which were traded online for 100-200 zloty each.

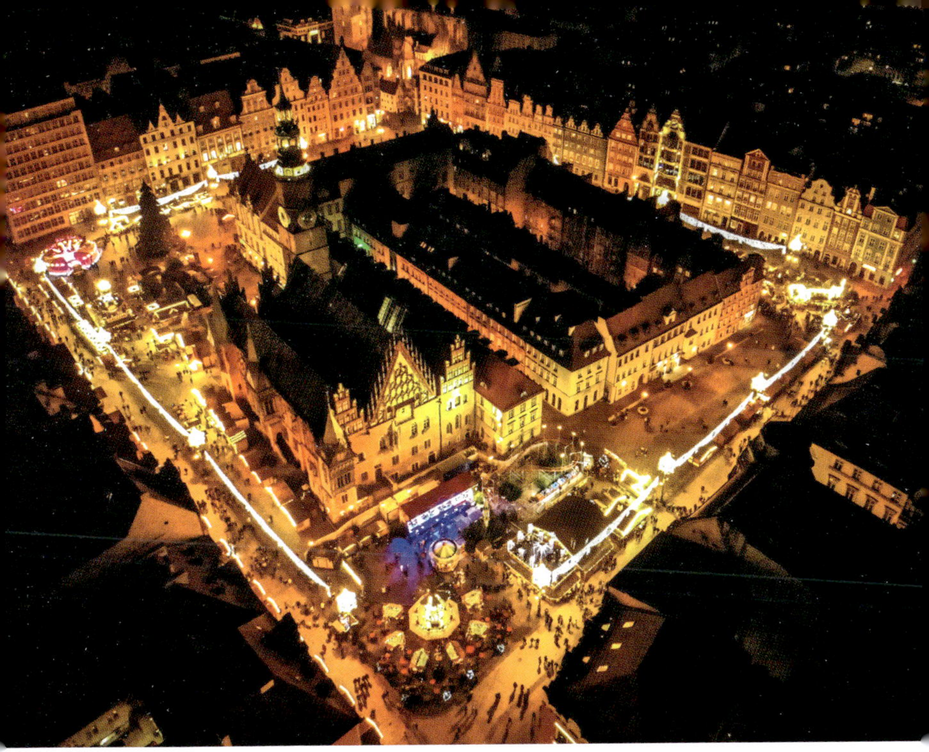

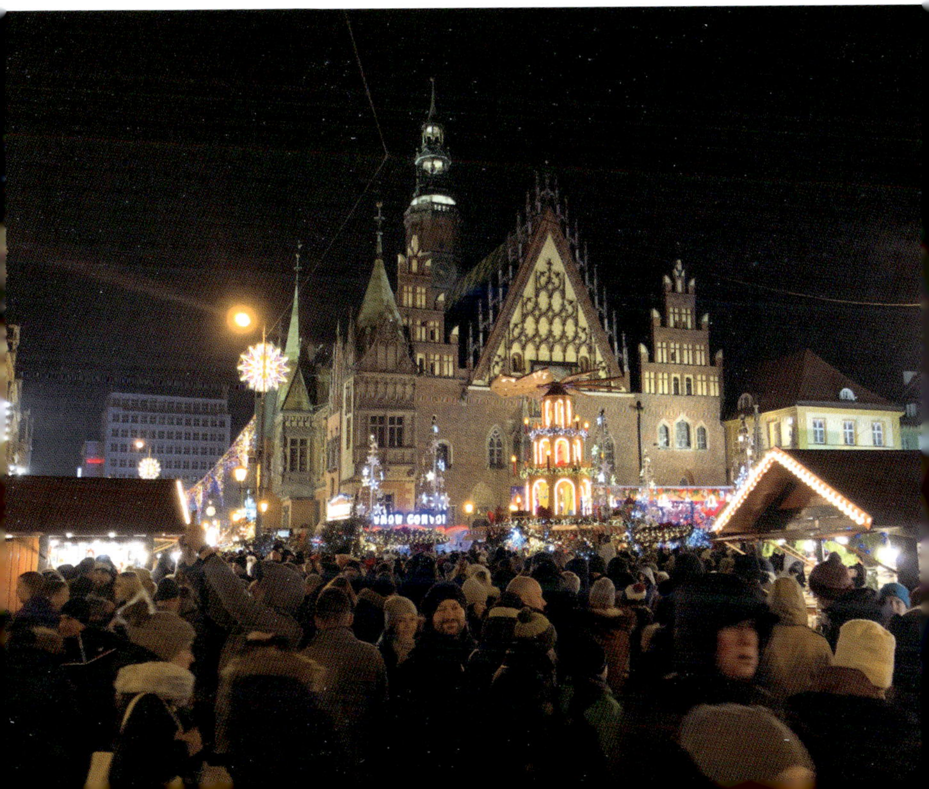

97 Wrocław's Main Railway Station
A fairytale castle or a railway station?

📍 D

- Piłsudskiego 105　🚆 Dworzec Główny　🕐 All year round　🇵🇱 Dworzec Główny
- Have a night out at the Railway Embankment (Nasyp) **75**

The main railway station also joins the list of superlatives associated with Wrocław and is certainly a must-see for visitors arriving by plane or car. Built between 1855 and 1857 to a design by Wilhelm Grapow, the architect of the Royal Upper Silesian Railway. One of the special features for a building from that time is the English Tudor style, which makes the station building look more like a fairytale castle. To this day, it is not entirely clear how the architect was able to assert himself with this unusual design, especially since Neo-Renaissance and Classicist constructions were predominant at the time. At the time, it was the largest railway station building in all of Germany!

From 1936 to 1939, there was a fast connection to Berlin – with the so-called „Flying Silesian" – that could be covered in less than three hours. Today, about 4.5 hours will need to be planned for this connection. But in addition to Berlin, there are now other international destinations that can be reached by night train, including Vienna, Budapest, Bratislava, and Kyiv.

The building was extensively renovated in 2010-2013 so it now appears almost in perfect condition. The entire area around it was extensively renovated and inviting terraces with colourful water features were created.

Due to its beautiful architecture, the station is often used as a film set. In 2019, this led to bizarre images when a documentary about the Second World War was filmed. For this purpose, huge flags with swastikas were hung up, although it was not immediately obvious that it was a film shoot. This caused a lot of confusion among the students just arriving for their first semester at the same time.

Another peculiarity is that this is one of the few railway stations in major Polish cities that has not yet been turned into a shopping centre. But don't worry – the closest one is right next door at the bus station.

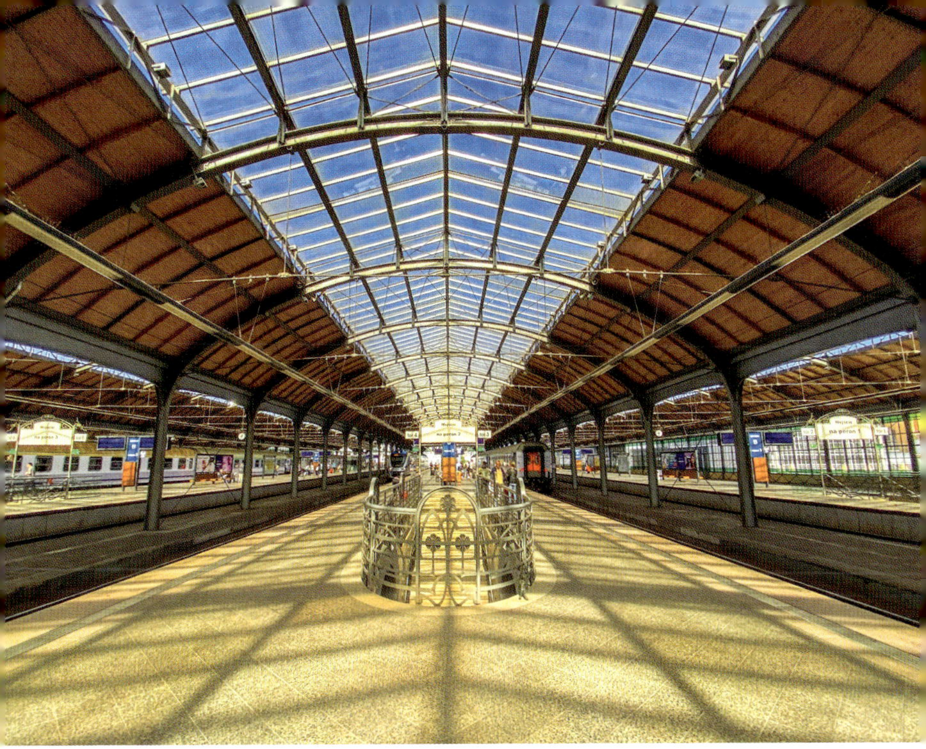

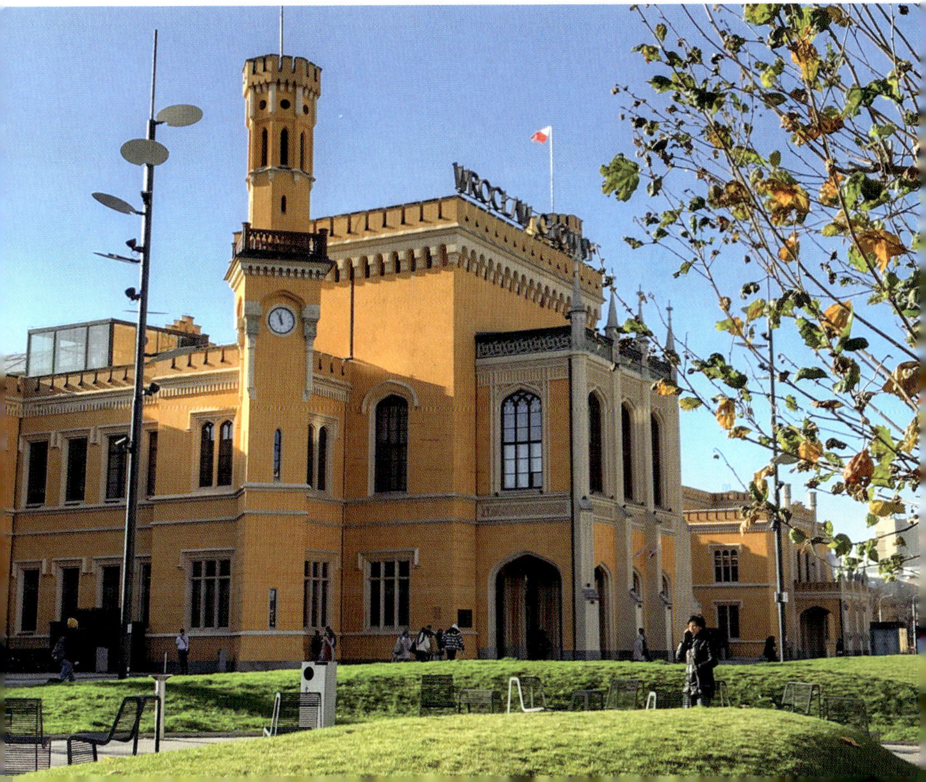

98 Xawery Dunikowski Promenade
The most beautiful views of Cathedral Island

🗺 D

🚋 Bulwar Xawerego Dunikowskiego 🚌 Hala Targowa 🕒 All year round
🚇 Bulwar Xawerego Dunikowskiego ⏩ Continue on to Partisan Hill **66**

While no longer a hidden gem, the promenade along the Oder river named after the artist Xawery Dunikowski – an Auschwitz survivor – is one of the most beautiful destinations for a stroll along the waterfront.

The starting point is the Market Hall next to Sand Bridge. The route follows the waterfront in the direction of Grunwaldzki Bridge. Right at the beginning, you'll pass one of the best places for panoramic photos – you won't find a more beautiful view of Cathedral Island with its skyline. The trees provide sufficient shade on hot summer days, and the fresh breeze provides some relief for visitors. A few steps further on, you'll reach the relaxing stair area with direct access to the water which was renovated a few years ago. To create some privacy, green spaces have been laid out between the steps. It's the perfect place for a romantic date – the sunset, which is visible here slowly reveals the shades of orange and red in the sky – almost guaranteeing success.

Kayaks and other boats can also moor here, and occasionally you'll see stand-up paddlers gliding on the river and enjoying the panorama from the water. Continuing towards Grunwaldzki Bridge, you'll pass a brick bastion, part of the former city fortifications built in 1585. When it was demolished in 1807, the bastion was transformed into a picturesque hill – another great photo spot.

Just two minutes from there is the Panorama Racławicka, a museum with only one painting – but it's 15 by 114 metres! It's an impressive panoramic painting depicting the victory of the Polish army over the Russians in the Battle of Racławice.

Along the entire promenade route, there are numerous seating areas and newly erected street food stalls that invite visitors to linger. However, many people simply visit Dunikowski Boulevard to read a book in peace and breathe in the surroundings. The promenade is not only suitable for pedestrians but also cyclists and scooter riders.

⚲ Shortly before the Grunwaldzki Bridge, you finally reach the National Museum. An imposing building in the Dutch neo-Renaissance style, once built to symbolise the power of a united Germany. Its full beauty is revealed in autumn, when the colouring of the leaves on the facade announces the end of the warm season.

99 Zajezdnia History Centre

A *An interactive place to understand Wrocław's post-war history*

Grabiszyńska 184 Bzowa (Centrum Zajezdnia) Tue+Wed 9–17h, Thu 10–17h, Fri–Sun 10–18h Centrum Historii Zajezdnia zajezdnia.org Get back into town, and maybe continue your day from the New Market Square **54**

Since the city was founded in the 10th century, the history of Wrocław has been complex and multifaceted. It's no wonder so many books have been written about all of its eras and various museums feature the city's history.

In the Zajezdnia History Centre, which opened in 2016, the focus is clearly on the events since 1945. On more than 1800 square metres of space in a former bus depot, the history of Wrocław after the end of the Second World War is presented in an interactive way. There is also a view of Silesia as a whole and of other Polish regions which, like Wrocław, were challenged greatly by the country's westward shift. Millions of people of many nationalities were affected by expulsion, and the history centre succeeds admirably in conveying the everyday life of the newly arrived city residents. Contemporary witnesses also provide information about their own fate via audio recording.

Fortunately, nobody needs to read a dusty history book to understand why the past left such clear marks on the present. There is also a separate section on the Solidarność movement and the so-called „Orange Alternative" - the anti-communist underground. These movements significantly contributed to the eventual fall of the Soviet Union and German reunification.

In the summer, the area next to the former bus depot is transformed into an open-air cinema that offers a colourful cultural programme on warm nights. But cinema lovers also get their money's worth in the winter, because the museum has a small cinema hall with a good 50 seats. In July 2022, an exhibition featured real Russian tanks which were destroyed by the Ukrainian Army after the unjustified invasion by Russia. It is always worth checking the website for the current programme.

100 Zwierzyniecki Bridge

📍 F

Fortunately, it escaped its destiny of being blown up

📍 Most Zwierzyniecki 🚊 Hala Stulecia 🕐 All year round
🔴 Most Zwierzyniecki we Wrocławiu ⏩ Visit the Centennial Hall **11**

The history of today's Zwierzyniecki Bridge, which is located near the Centennial Hall and the Zoo, dates back as far as 1655. Back then, it was only a simple wooden construction, but it served its purpose. In 1704, the bridge was officially named *most Przepustkowy* (Pass Bridge). Contrary to what one might expect, however, no border or customs control took place there. Instead, visitors to the city were tested for contagious diseases on arrival – after all, a few decades earlier the city had been hit by the plague and lost half of its population to it.

Named Zwierzyniecki Bridge since the end of the war, this overpass is a showpiece of bridge art and – along with Grunwaldzki Bridge – probably one of the most beautiful bridges in the city. It was built between 1895 and 1897 based on a design by Karl Klimm and Richard Plüddemann. In 2022, another renovation took place to transform the bridge's modern yellow color back to its original green, maroon and black scheme.

The 62-metre-long and 21.8-metre-wide bridge holds a record: it is the oldest bridge in the city that is passable by cars and has been in continuous use since its completion! It is only thanks to an extremely fortunate circumstance that the bridge was not destroyed during the war. In the last days of the war, during the Siege of Breslau, it was expected that there would be attacks from the east. The bridge had already been prepared with explosives, but the attack came from a different direction, and one of the most beautiful Oder bridges was saved from being blown up.

From the water, there is an interesting perspective on the bridge with its neo-baroque decorative elements. At the small pier right next door, kayaks, and pedal boats are rented in the summer – and combined they make an ideal romantic setting.

Bonus Chapter: What do others say?

Old and new residents of Wrocław reveal their three favourite places.

Why is it always the authors who have their say in travel guides? We want to break with that tradition here. After all, the diversity of Wrocław's residents is just as exciting as the city itself.

That's why some of the people living in Wrocław are presenting their favourite places here. Not just personalities who are closely connected to the city, but also a few randomly selected Wrocław residents reveal their three very personal favourite places.

Rafał Dutkiewicz

As the long-time mayor of Wrocław (2002-2018), Rafał Dutkiewicz left his mark on the city's history like no other during his years in office. He has also repeatedly supported human rights and promoted having an open mindset far beyond the city limits. During his time in office, Wrocław experienced an investment boom, more than 160,000 new direct jobs were created and the city's per capita gross domestic product even doubled. Here he reveals his three personal favourite places in Wrocław. Those who think city hall is an obvious choice might be surprised...

💛 The „Concordia Design" on Słodowa Island (building no. 7)

There are a couple of places with magnificent views of Wrocław: the Mathematical Tower in the building of the University of Wrocław, the tower of St. Elizabeth's Church, or from the spires of the Wrocław Cathedral.

But nothing compares to the view from the roof terrace of building number 7 on Słodowa Island, where the „Concordia Design" is located and a bar is open to the public.

The silver Nawa sculpture by Oskar Zięta, the Oder River flowing along the building of the Ossolineum and Wrocław University, the lanterns along ul. Grodzka, the Baroque sculpture of the University Church, the Gothic silhouette of the Greek Catholic Cathedral...

Magical places. A magical sight.

💛 The Archdiocesan Museum on Cathedral Island (Book Henryków)

There are two UNESCO lists: on the one hand, there is the list of World Heritage Sites with the most magnificent urban and architectural works as well as natural monuments. The Centennial Hall is on this list. The second list, the so-called World Documentary Heritage, lists the most important documents in world history.

Wrocław was the European Capital of Culture in 2016 — and the World Book Capital in 2017. This year, at our suggestion, The Book of Henryków (Księga Henrykowska) was included in the World Document Heritage List.

The book was written near Wrocław and is a diary from the 13th century kept by a German monk. In it, he quotes in Latin the sentence of a Czech peasant speaking in Polish to his Polish wife: „Let me, I shall grind, and you take a rest." (Day, ut ia pobrusa, a ti poziwai.)

This is the first sentence in Polish. This is Silesia. A German writing in Latin quotes a sentence from a Czech-speaking Polish man to his Polish wife.

The Book of Henryków can be found in the Archdiocesan Museum (Muzeum Archidiecezji Wrocławskiej) on Cathedral Island next to the Wrocław Cathedral and the Church of the Holy Cross (Kościoł św Krzyża), whose canon was Nicolaus Copernicus.

· ·

💛 The Greek Catholic Church of St. Vincent

This is a Greek-Catholic cathedral in the city centre (Katedra greckokatolicka pw św. Wincentego i św. Jakuba). A magnificent Gothic temple with a beautiful iconostasis in front of the main altar. The icons were written by the master of Eastern icon painting, Jerzy Nowosielski. Gothic and icons. West and East.

The Hochberg Chapel is „attached" to the church. The commissioner for its construction at the beginning of the 18th century was Count Ferdinand von Hochberg, abbot of the Premonstratensian monastery, who decided to prepare a place for his burial there. He competed in the show off of wealth with those on the neighbouring Cathedral Island. Therefore, rich gilding and lots of baroque splendour were used. The chapel was demolished during the last phase of the war — one of the many casualties of the Wrocław fortress (Festung Breslau) — but was recently rebuilt with municipal and European funds. A great stroke of luck, considering that the stone carving above the altar had to be reassembled from 1,300 pieces — it had broken into so many fragments during the war.

St Vincent's Church, where the end of the war and the new Europe, East and West, Gothic and Baroque styles meet, is getting busier and busier — not least because over 100,000 Ukrainian citizens have settled in Wrocław in recent years. They came here to work, but also out of fear of the war in their home country. In my opinion, this is the new, great face of Wrocław in the 21st century: almost 200,000 new residents from 124 different countries have arrived since the turn of the millennium. Before our eyes, the Silesian metropolis is transforming from an ethnically homogeneous into an international city.

Hans Jörg Neumann

led the German Consulate General in Wrocław from 2018 to 2022, which, together with the branch office in Opole, is one of the largest German general consulates in the world. After spending several years in Cairo, Prague, Washington, Bucharest, Cotonou, and Los Angeles, he quickly took Wrocław into his heart. His three favourite places:

💛 **The observation tower of the Elizabeth Church.** I usually take all my guests up there to enjoy the most beautiful panoramic view of the city. But you have to earn it first: there are over 300 steps to climb. The other viewpoints are, of course, also breathtaking, such as the view from Wrocław Cathedral, but the panorama from the Elizabeth Church is simply something very special.

💛 **The view from my living room of the cycle path and walkway on the banks of the Oder,** from Biskupiński Park towards Bartoszowicki Bridge. I love the hustle and bustle there, especially on Sunday afternoons when there are lots of families and cyclists. Word of this hidden gem seems to have spread far already… Especially the lock and the two weirs, together with the beach bars where passing cyclists like to stop for a beer, make up a great atmosphere on the waterfront.

💛 **The Afrykarium in the Wrocław Zoo.** For me, this is „Erste Bundesliga" (first division) and really something quite extraordinary. There you can see ecosystems from the African continent, where, for example, you walk in a glass tunnel through the middle of one of the numerous aquariums — surrounded by sharks, rays, and other exciting fish species. I am convinced that this will excite a much wider audience than just animal lovers and children!

Arne Franke

🌐 www.arnefranke.de
📷 arnefranke.studienreisen

As an architectural historian and author, he is fascinated by the city and its diverse architecture — from Romanesque to Habsburg Baroque and Prussian Classicism to the Classical Modernism of the 1920s and Socialist Modernism after 1945. On his study tours, he regularly leads interested groups through Silesian architectural history.

・・

💛 **The UNESCO World Heritage Site of the Centennial Hall** by Max Berg, **the Four Dome Pavilion** by Poelzig, and the adjacent **WuWa** housing estate from 1929: the first two buildings because they introduce Classical Modernism before the „Bauhaus", and the WuWa housing estate because it embodies the efficiency of Silesian architects.

・・

💛 **The Market Square** with its partly rebuilt patrician houses, the magnificent late-gothic town hall, and the adjacent St. Elizabeth Church, which, with its funerary monuments is a pantheon of the Wrocław patrician class. And the fascinating university building with the preserved „Aula Leopoldina". And, and, and...

・・

💛 **The City Museum** in the former „Palais Spaetgen", later the Prussian royal palace. Not only has the restoration and reconstruction of the historic interiors been successful here, but the museum collection and the conception of the presentation are also outstanding and offer an excellent introduction to the history of the city, as well as Silesian regional history.

Iza Mularonek & Agata Szczasny

🌐 www.wroclawkobiecymokiem.pl
📷 wroclawkobiecymokiem
📘 www.facebook.com/wroclawkobiecymokiem

Iza has walked all of Wrocław. A bit out of a need to explore and a bit out of an aversion to crowds, she always chooses the less frequented streets and paths. She is enchanted by pre-war Wrocław, the old photographs, the wooden doors, the dusty tiles, and the history shyly peeking out from under the plaster. She loves the mysteries of this city, its tenements, streets, and people. She is sure that one day, by complete chance, she will discover one of them or find some treasure.

Agata was drawn to Wrocław from the east by love. At the time, she thought it would be for a while, to study. But it turned out that Wrocław stole her heart for good. Since 1999, she has been discovering that this is her place on earth every day. She loves photography. Thousands of captured frames allow her to forever record places, events, people, and the feelings accompanying her at any given moment.

Together they have a blog called Wrocław with a Woman's Eye *(Wrocław Kobiecym Okiem)* where they showcase everything that is beautiful, tasty, interesting, and worth knowing about Wrocław. They recently published the first, subjective, alternative, non-obvious, living guide to Wrocław *(Wrocław. Kierunkowy 71)*. Their aim is to make people fall in love with Wrocław. Professionally, they run the advertising agency Niezły Team, which creates, develops, and supports brands and places in the HoReCa and IT industry.

💛 **Radio RAM,** as it has always accompanied us, every day. A Wrocław radio station with the best music, a large dose of local news, the absurd competitions we love, and the voices that put a smile on our faces. Piotr Bartyś, Maciek Przestalski, Ania Fluder, and once Monika Jaworska have become part of our lives.

💛 **Neon Gallery** — the most Instagrammed place in Wrocław. At night, lit up with a million colours. Always teeming with life. A beautiful piece of Wrocław's history in one place.

💛 **Opatowicki weir (Jaz Opatowicki)** — Wrocław wouldn't be the same without the Oder River. It is on the Opatowicki weir where we like this river the most. The murmur of the water is magical there and the surroundings invite you to take a walk and relax.

Amit Chandra

🌐 www.whistlinghound.com
📷 whistlinghound
📘 www.facebook.com/whistlinghound

is a digital marketer, travel writer, and tour guide who has lived in Wrocław since completing his studies. He shares his experiences and discoveries on his blog and social media, aptly complemented by his pictures. Follow him on Instagram for some incredible sunset pictures of Wrocław. If you want to learn more about the most fascinating winter hikes in Lower Silesia, unique finds in and around Wrocław, and much more, we recommend visiting his blog.

💛 **Aula Leopoldina** is the finest Baroque work in Wrocław and among the best in Poland. Stand in the middle of this stunning hall oozing with medieval charm and you'll be amazed by the sheer perfection of the artwork — the result of several years of work. I recommend everyone to visit here.

💛 **Park Grabiszyński** is the most scenic and lush park in Wrocław, with some old trees towering over the park pathways. The park looks dreamy with all its autumn colours.

💛 **Zalew „Bajkał"** — Wrocław has its own Bajkał lake, literally in the middle of nowhere. Some 15 km southeast of the Wrocław city centre, Bajkał thrives in peace and tranquillity and is the perfect nature escape. You can camp, swim, barbecue, fish, or spend a lazy weekend chilling on a hammock by the lakefront.

Christian A. Dumais

🌐 www.cadumais.com
📘 facebook.com/cadumais
🐦 📷 PuffChrissy

is an American writer, editor, and comedian who has lived in Wrocław for almost 20 years and is proud to call the city his home.

💛 **Las Mokrzański (Mokrzański Forest)**
Located on the western outskirts of the city, this na-

tional forest is a beautiful place to get lost in for an afternoon. With lots of paths to choose from, the possibilities for hiking and biking feel endless. You can park your car and start at the entrance at Teofila Modelskiego and head south to Leśnica (where a castle awaits you, as well as some local coffee and pastries), or you can wander north to Wilkszyn (where coffee also awaits you — hey, I like my coffee!). Personally, I love riding my bike there and discovering things deep in the woods (like the Blair Witch-like remains of the once-prominent Waldschlößchen restaurant).

💛 **Uniwersytet Przyrodniczy we Wrocławiu** (Wrocław University of Environmental and Life Sciences)
Whenever I'm in the area, I always take a detour through this campus. Specifically, starting at the main entrance off of ul. Norwida because I love the slightly disorienting feeling of how the persistent noise of the city disappears as you walk through the large entryway. Once you're on the other side, wander toward the left to enjoy some varying architectural styles as this university collides with the neighboring medical university. Keep walking for the real treat though: depending on the day, you're going to see horses, chickens, dogs, pigs, sheep, and more. It's not just a mental break from the hustle and bustle of the city — it's a free zoo.

💛 **Cegielnia Stabłowicka** — The city renovated this lake a few years ago by adding a pathway — with wooden bridges — that circles the whole body of water along with benches and plenty of fishing spots. It's a lovely spot to relax and walk your dog. And if you enjoy fishing, there are local competitions and overnight fishing/camping events.

Tomek

🌐 www.freewalkingtour.com
📷 freewalkativetour

is not only a travel guide but also a professional optimist.

💛 **All the islands and bridges in general** — the city has so many islands connected by a huge number of bridges. I love the atmosphere of the promenades as much as discovering new beautiful shores of the Oder River or a new bridge far outside the city.

💛 **The Church of St. Michael** (Kościół pw św Michała Archanioła) in Ołbin. The magical, gloomy, neo-Gothic church with its comical asymmetrical towers reminds me of romantic stories from the 19th century. The surroundings with the park and the preserved pre-war buildings trigger a nice melancholic feeling in me.

💛 **The railway embankment (Nasyp),** located in the centre near the station, with its numerous pubs. Unlike many other constructions near the station, this one has a unifying effect on the city and its inhabitants.

Ari

is a film producer and amateur musician who came to Wrocław eight years ago through a chain of coincidences. Above all, he thinks the people in Wrocław are cool and says it's easy to make connections here.

💛 **Rowerownia CRK** — a place where you can get professional help for bicycle repairs. The numerous tools can be used for free or for a symbolic price.

💛 **Bar Pierożek**, because it not only has the best selection of delicious pierogi, but the prices are also fair. Moreover, the bar is hardly known among tourists and therefore rarely crowded.

💛 **Tamka** — a paradise for artists. Great parties, rehearsal rooms for musicians, and well managed overall.

Siobhain

came to Wrocław from England to work as a teacher here.

💛 **Semafor** for the huge portions of tasty food at a great value. The decor is like a train, which is really cool.

💛 **Nietota**, especially on Saturday evenings. It's great fun to dance there to the old 80s and 90s classics.

💛 Right in front of my flat. Why? I'll never get bored of looking directly at a **train station** that looks like a fairytale castle!

Johannes

There is only one thing Johannes prefers over his synthesizers: the summer vibes in Wrocław. Love led him to the city and new friendships kept him here.

💛 **Słodowa Island,** of course! A great concept, just giving the party people a place to drink their beer in peace, eat snacks, try out slacklining, or even meet the love of their life.

💛 **Café Kalambur.** The living room of artists and hipsters, with the smallest gallery in Poland. A cosy cave for a tipsy afternoon nap in winter and always the first choice for Tinder dates.

💛 **The Sunday Świebodzki flea market** — Wrocław's little version of Marrakesh. Visit it quickly before the hipsters move in. Here you can get homemade cakes, Haribos in huge quantities, or fresh apples from a Polish grandmother's garden.

Kamila

📷 follow_my_feet_in_wroclove

was born in Wrocław, then spent 18 years away before coming back to study and staying. When she's not working at the university, she's exploring the old tenement buildings from pre-war times and especially their tiles — recognisable from her Instagram profile, which she herself describes as monothematic.

💛 **Plac Mordechaja Anielewicza,** which was called Eichendorffplatz before the war. I only discovered it by chance. It's beautiful and exudes a very special atmosphere. The square was built in the late 1920s/early 1930s in a neighbourhood with many villas, which clearly stand out from the boxy villa architecture of today. It is located at the intersection of three streets — instead of buildings, there is a small park with a pond and fountain in the middle. A beautiful ensemble of different trees creates a unique microclimate. The pond is also very popular with ducks — as a breeding ground!

💛 **The city's National Museum.** The building is not only historic and home to great exhibitions. It is also home to my favourite painting — the portrait of Maryna Parenska, painted by Stanisław Wyspiański in 1903.

💛 The entire streets of **ul. Norwida** and **ul. Curie-Sklodowskiej.** I work there, and you can also find the most beautiful residential buildings and, above all, the most magnificent floors in the city!

Giulia

🌐 www.mondomulia.com
📷 mondomulia

is a blogger and photographer who has been sharing her adventures in travel and food on her blog Mondomulia and Instagram since 2011. Born in Rome, Giulia has spent nearly half her life living in other cities around the world...until she fell in love with Wrocław and Poland! When she's not at home baking cakes to share with friends or abroad exploring a new country, you will find Giulia in one of Wrocław's many specialty coffee shops.

💛 As a coffee lover, it's important for me to live in a city with a vibrant and growing specialty coffee culture. There are so many wonderful cafés and independent roasters in Wrocław, but if I had to pick one, it would be **OTO Coffee Bar.** Why? Great location in a lively street, talented baristas, and delicious coffee served in beautiful handmade ceramic cups!

💛 In spring, there is no place more beautiful than the **Botanical Garden,** when so many plants are blooming. Although it's right next to one of the most touristy places (Cathedral Island), the garden is a quiet place to relax, read a book or chat with friends on a cozy bench. Definitely a hidden gem in the city!

💛 One of the (many) things I love about Wrocław is that you can easily get around by bike. On weekends, I love to cycle along the Oder River, crossing bridges and exploring the city's islands, parks, and beaches. My favourite area for cycling is **Szczytnicki Park,** with a stop at Mała Czarna for a flat white or at Przełam Lody for gelato!

Nastia

 www.facebook.com/lookinarts/
 nastiachernica

moved from Moscow to Wrocław to study and stayed right here. She is a part-time artist, part-time boat captain, but a full-time lover of adventure.

💛 **The whole Nadodrze neighbourhood** — undoubtedly the most exciting and authentic area of the city. You can quickly lose yourself in the colourful street art and the numerous small cafés and bars, or just admire the old tenement houses from pre-war times and enjoy a walk through history.

💛 **The Oder River!** What exactly is there to explain? A place for all year round, but, of course, especially in summer, when it's time to go out with friends for a boat trip — or alternatively by kayak or stand-up paddle.

💛 **Park Południowy** — the only park in the city that is really completely new. A perfect choice for an afternoon stroll, a lazy weekend on the grass, meeting friends, an evening date, a bike ride to watch birds, and any other outdoor activity. I love working on new ideas there with my sketchbook!

Klaudia

 panda.tort

bakes what are probably the best cakes in town, but according to her, only when she's bored. In any case, her Instagram account will make you hungry.

💛 **Staromiejski Park,** because it's simply the most beautiful park in the city and the carousel there is just great!

💛 **The zoo.** I could spend the whole day there and it still wouldn't be enough!

💛 **Paper Concept** — a little craft shop for people who like to be artistic. Whenever I'm there, the hours fly by…

Karolina

🌐 www.wanderlust.com.pl/

When she's not at work or writing new articles for her travel blog, she whizzes around the city on inline skates. But she may have been wearing shoes when she discovered her three favourite places:

💛 **"Tor Wrotkarski"**, a running track, especially for inline skating. Definitely the best place for people with this hobby! Right next door is Tysiąclecia Park, which is wonderful for relaxing afterward.

💛 **Woo Thai Street Food** — if you like Thai cuisine and especially spicy food, this is the place to go. The tastiest Pad Thai in Wrocław!

💛 **Forma Płynna beach bar** — on the north bank of the Polinka cable car and centrally located, with definitely the best hammocks in town.

Malwina

likes to go in search of the city's unusual but inspiring places.

💛 For all animal lovers, the two cafés — **Parrot Coffee** (with parrots) or **Kot Café** (with cats) — are ideal places to go. You can enjoy your coffee in the best company!

💛 **Zielona Oliwka in Kiełczów** — it's not directly in the city, but it's definitely worth a visit. The food is fantastic and families with children will feel right at home, as there is a pond with picnic facilities, a huge playground, and a petting zoo.

💛 **KFC Rynek Świdnicka** — this is the place where you can meet many interesting people, especially after midnight, when you are coming back home from a party or just want to eat something warm at night. My friends and I always say that the best meetings happens at this KFC.

Jacek Sterczewski

🌐 www.lokietka5.pl

works as a coordinator at Infopunkt Łokietka 5, an organisation active in the Nadodrze neighbourhood, networking and supporting the artists, shops, residents, and restaurants there. He enjoys spending his time at the numerous cultural events in Wrocław and exploring the city by bike. Here are his favourite places:

💛 **The Food Think Tank** — a café with lots of positive energy, great art, and plenty of sunshine. An absolutely natural meeting place in the heart of Nadodrze.

💛 **Niskie Łąki Park** — a quiet and green area in the immediate vicinity of the Oławskie suburb. In addition to the colourful hustle and bustle of wildlife along the Oława River, a spectacular art installation by Joanna Rajkowska called „Trafostacja" can also be seen there.

💛 **The entire ul. Świdnicka** and the cityscape from this perspective. If you follow the street north from the Market Square, you will see all the architectural eras in Wrocław at once: from Barbara to the National Music Forum to the Renoma department stores, and Kościuszki Square.

Maciej Wlazło

📘 www.facebook.com/wroclawskabroda/
📷 beardofbreslau

loves to search for traces of Wrocław's past, such as old inscriptions hidden on the walls of pre-war houses, as well as in courtyards and stairways. He not only leads city walks with this particular thematic focus but is also active online as the „Beard of Wrocław".

💛 **The old city harbour** — one of the last post-industrial buildings with a history of over a hundred years. A place hardly frequented by locals or tourists. Not only do many interesting photographic objects await you there, but the Oder also radiates peace and tranquillity in the harbour basin.

💛 **The courtyards in the Przedmieście Oławskie** — a neighbourhood with a dubious reputation, but definitely unjustified. The only place in Wrocław with so many temples and places of worship of various denominations and churches. Beautiful old houses with interesting staircases, but also whole labyrinths of courtyards with relics of old factories and industrial plants. It reminds me a little bit of the Praga district in Warsaw.

💛 **Park Wschodni on the eastern outskirts of Wrocław.** It was originally designed as a recreation area for the residents of Oławskie. From the air, it looks like a fish. In addition to the recreational and sports facilities, the park also holds memories from the time of war and unrest — from the 1930s and 1940s, but also from the era when the traces of Wrocław's former inhabitants were removed.

Adrian

🌐 use-it.eu/cities/detail/wroclaw
👤 www.facebook.com/useit.wroclaw

moved to Wrocław from Portugal thirteen years ago and „suffers" from FOMO („fear of missing out"). Therefore, not only does he often attend numerous events, but he is also very culturally active, organizing secret concerts, movie discussions, cooking exchanges, etc. Currently, he is working on an alternative city map of Wrocław, as part of the USE-IT Europe initiative.

💛 Clearly **the Czajownia Tea House** (Herbaciarnia Czajownia). Although it's right in the city centre, no noise makes its way inside and you can really relax there. They know a lot about teas and have the best backyard garden!

💛 **Kalambur/Kalaczakra**: two pubs in one. One rock-style area for smokers, where usually a lot of alcohol flows, and the other has tea and a relaxed atmosphere. Even though it is well-known and popular, there is simply no better place to experience the local cultural scene, with free concerts almost every week.

💛 **Park Leśnicki** — On the western city limits, it is a beautiful park with an old castle that is also an active cultural centre. Perfect for a weekend walk. concerts almost every week.

Kasia

🌐 www.mieszkaniewkamienicy.com
📷 mieszkaniewkamienicy

explores the many pre-war houses in Wrocław and shares her love for them with readers of her blog. In 2019, she also launched a project in which volunteers use simple methods and only a few hours of their time to pragmatically restore such houses to a better condition. Sometimes it's just enough to remove some graffiti and sweep a little dust off the decorative elements.

💛 **The flea market at the old mill!** A place where you can travel back in time and find great vintage objects that will quickly take you back to the old days of the People's Republic of Poland and the former Wrocław.

💛 **The Przedmieście Oławskie** — the perfect area to simply stroll through the streets and explore old architecture. Here you will find countless surprises, stunning tiles, ornaments, and staircases. All you have to do is open the beautifully decorated doors and you can immediately enter the magical world of pre-war houses.

💛 **All the green spaces in the city** — especially those close to cafés and restaurants! The Botanical Garden is just a few steps away from Restaurant Ragu, and the city moat (old city promenade) is right by Vaffa Napoli. To get to the Oder River, walk through the garden of the Ossolineum, but, of course, stop at Vinyl Café first.

Ewa

loves to explore the city's history with all its facets.

💛 **The hydroelectric power station** on the Oder River, right on the northern edge of the old town. It was designed by Max Berg and Günther Trauer and is proof that industrial buildings don't have to be boring and ugly.

💛 **The New Horizons Cinema.** I am a big fan of cinematography and this cinema really leaves nothing to be desired. A great selection of films even beyond the box office hits, great festivals, and a cool atmosphere.

💛 **Lody Roma!** The best ice cream parlour I know. There's not much to explain, but make sure you try the „black sesame" (czarny sezam) flavour!

Marina

says that Wrocław combines the characteristics of two of her favourite cities — Berlin and Lviv. The city is exciting, diverse, and at the same time very cosy.

💛 **The Tajne Komplety** bookshop, which is also a chess club, café, and dance floor. There are also coworking spaces — half of my thesis was written there.

💛 **The EkoBazar at the Mieszczański Brewery,** which takes place every Saturday. I love it for its great pancakes and good coffee.

💛 **The Hala Targowa** market hall because it's full of small cafés and kiosk stalls. Fresh fruit and vegetables are there too, of course!

María

moved to Wrocław from Venezuela for a job and, like so many others, stayed because of the city.

💛 My personal number one is definitely **the historic Market Square** and the whole area. It's beautiful and there are always new details to discover!

💛 **Cathedral Island.** It is full of history and breathtaking architecture and should be part of every visitor's must-see programme. And not only during the day! The island is also a great place to visit in the later evening hours!

💛 **The Wroclavia Shopping Centre** near the train station. It's modern and cosy in design, with lots of contemporary shops and a wide variety!

Mirko

Although he has already written about 100 extraordinary places in the main section, he cannot resist quickly adding three personal favourites:

💛 **The north bank of the Oder,** especially the view of the „Jaz Różanka" weir from the island path (ul. Pasterska) between Most Osobowicki and Most Trzebnicki. Dreamlike sunsets can be watched from this point and the sound of the water from the weir, coupled with a fresh breeze, makes this a magical place — especially with the autumn leaves.

💛 The mural by French artist Guillaume Alby (known as Remed) on a vacant house on **ul. Ptasia.** It shows an illustration of a man who has a chopped off right hand and a heart above his left hand. Remy wrote many years later that he remembered the somewhat „sketchy" area well, but where the people were so friendly…

💛 **The Oder River in the city centre** between the Sikorskiego and Pomorska bridges. The first one has a small staircase on its north side leading down to the water. There you are rewarded with a great view of Max Berg's hydroelectric power station and the former All Saints Hospital complex — now the new old town boulevard (Bulwar Staromiejski).

City Plan

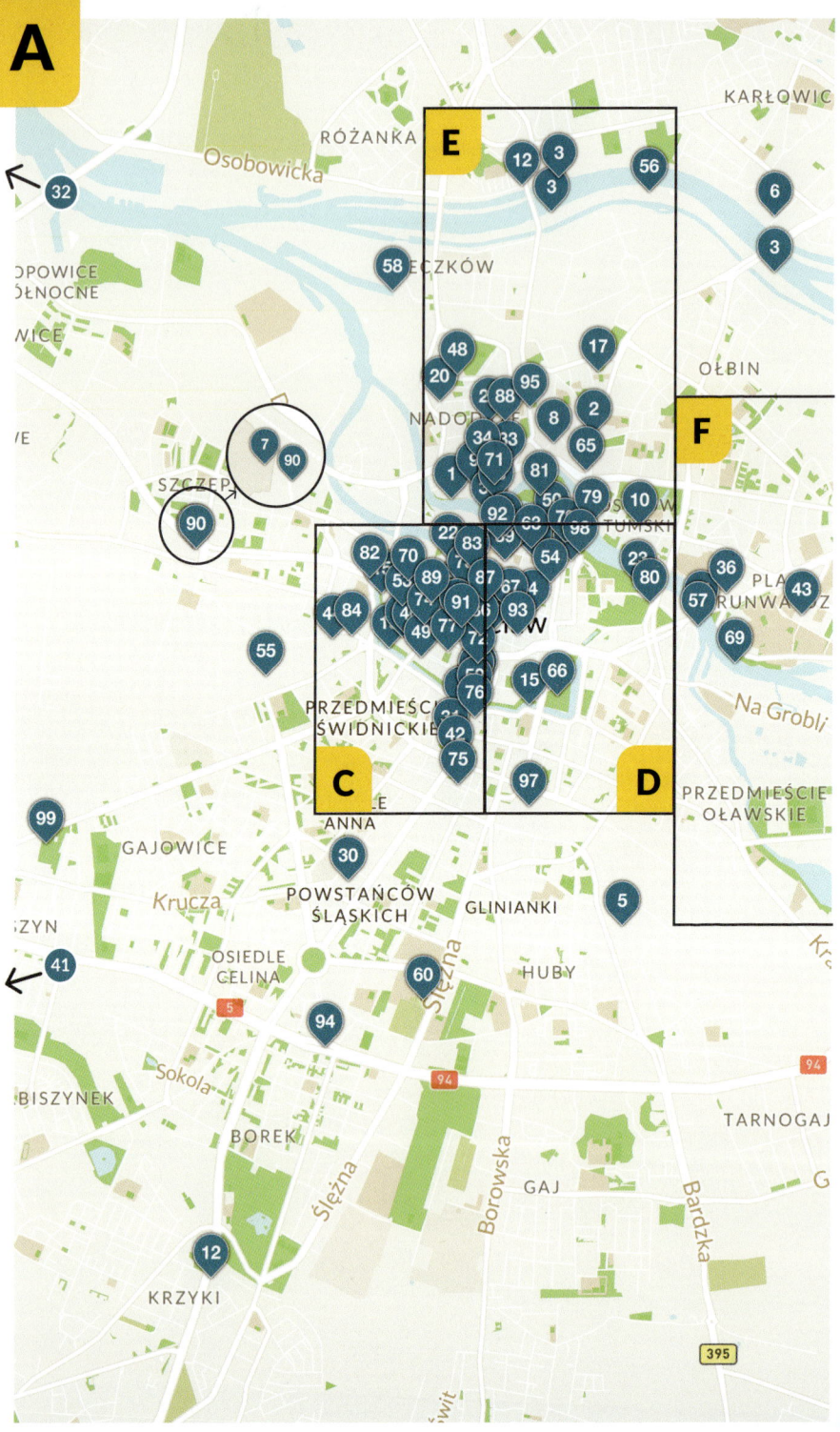

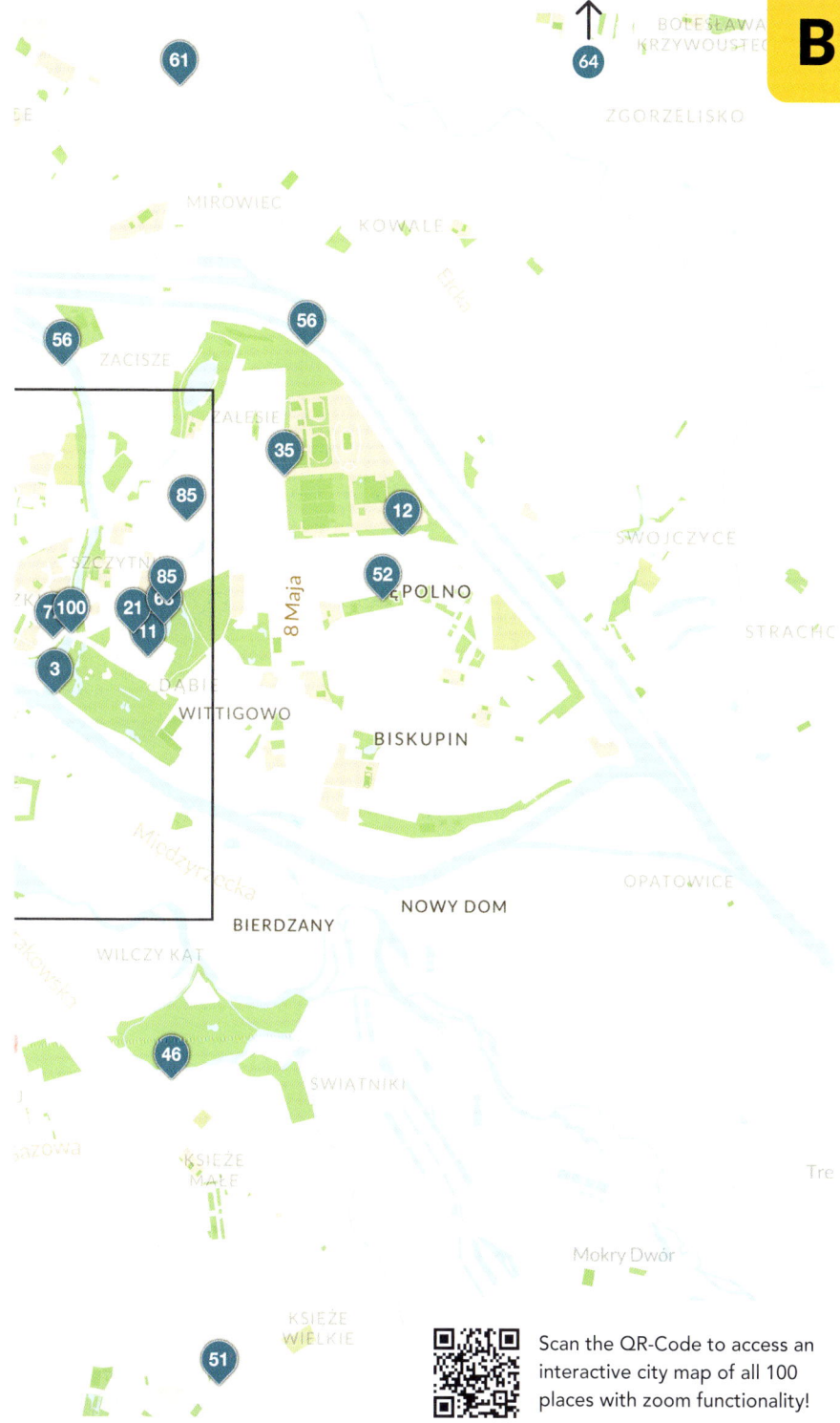

Scan the QR-Code to access an interactive city map of all 100 places with zoom functionality!

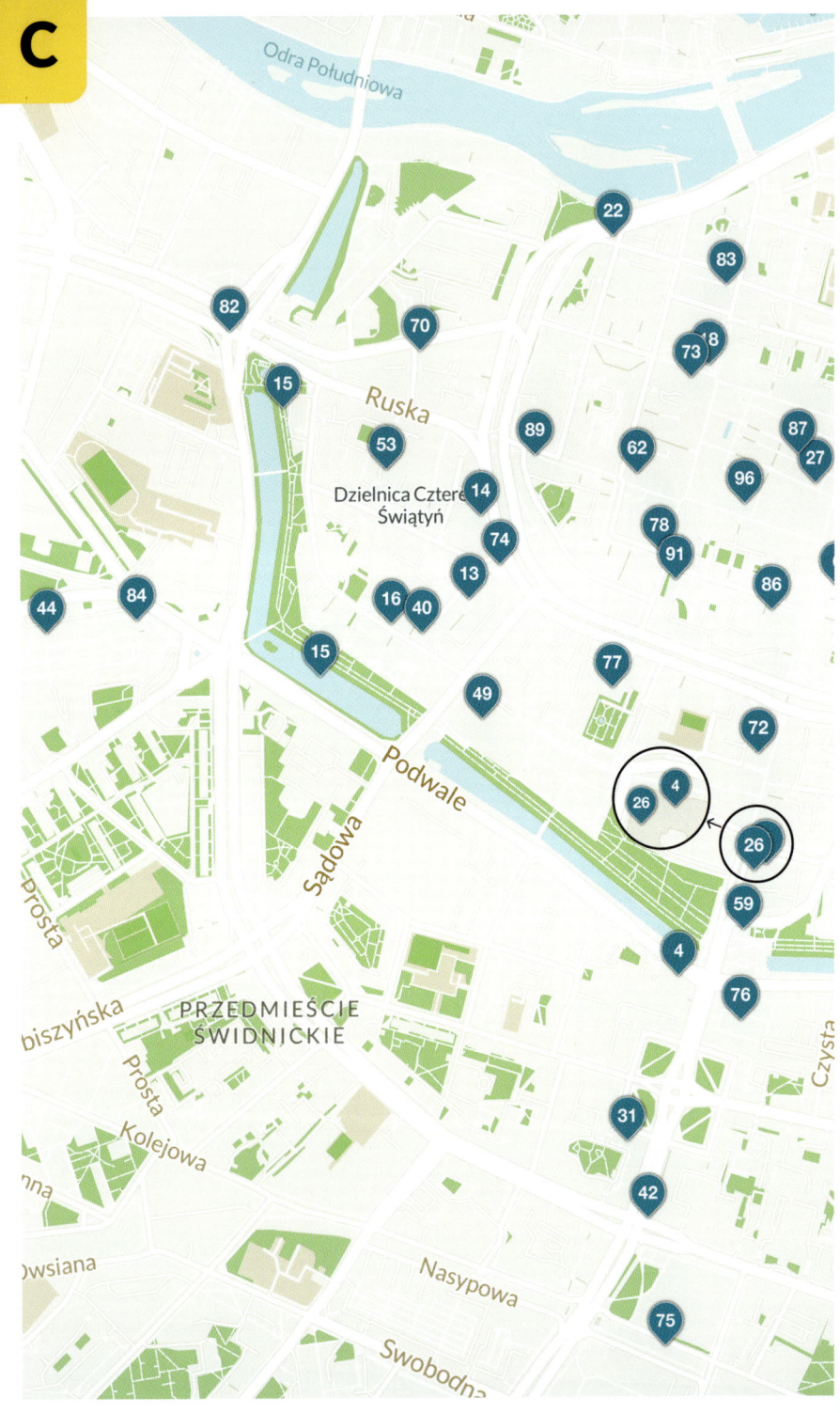

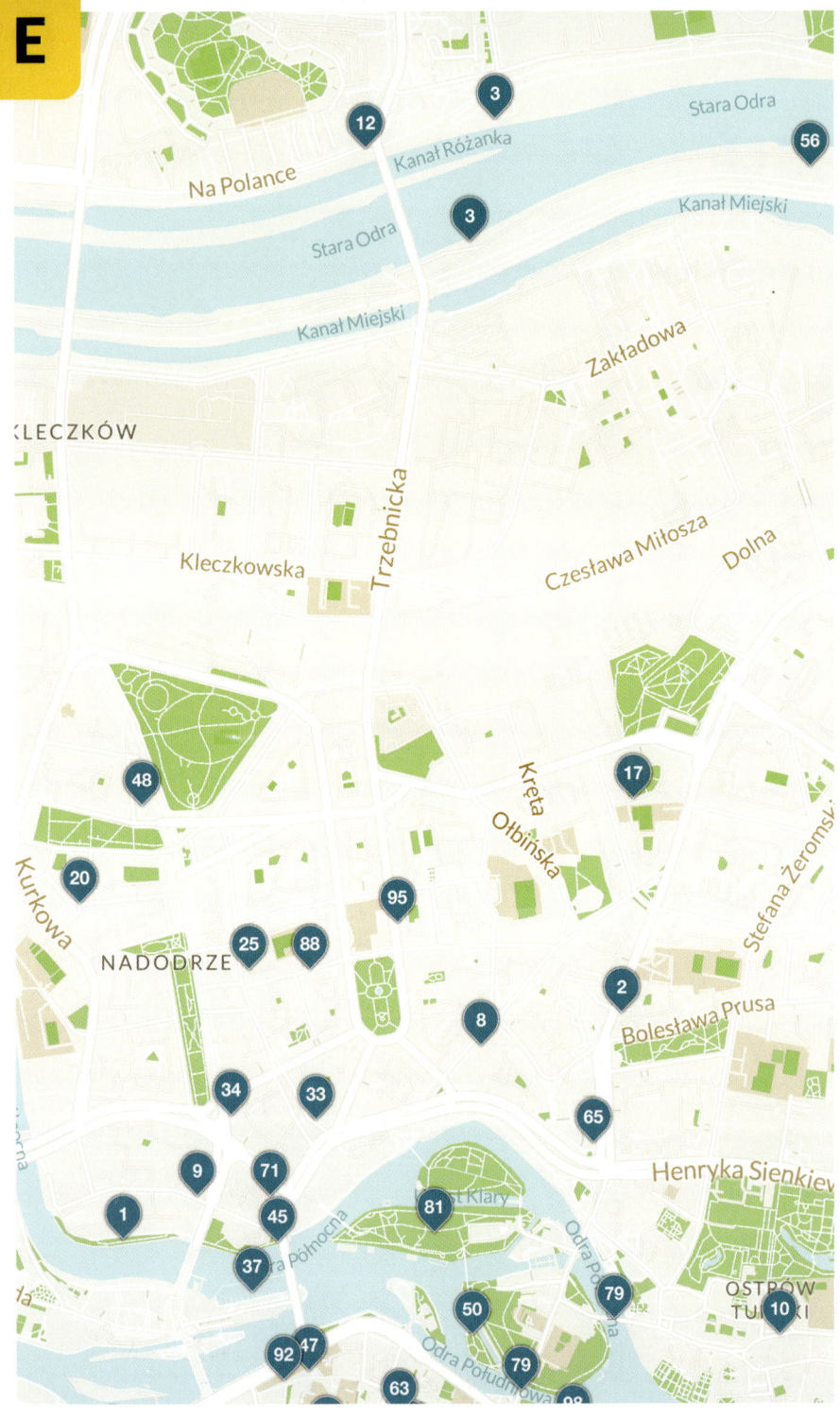

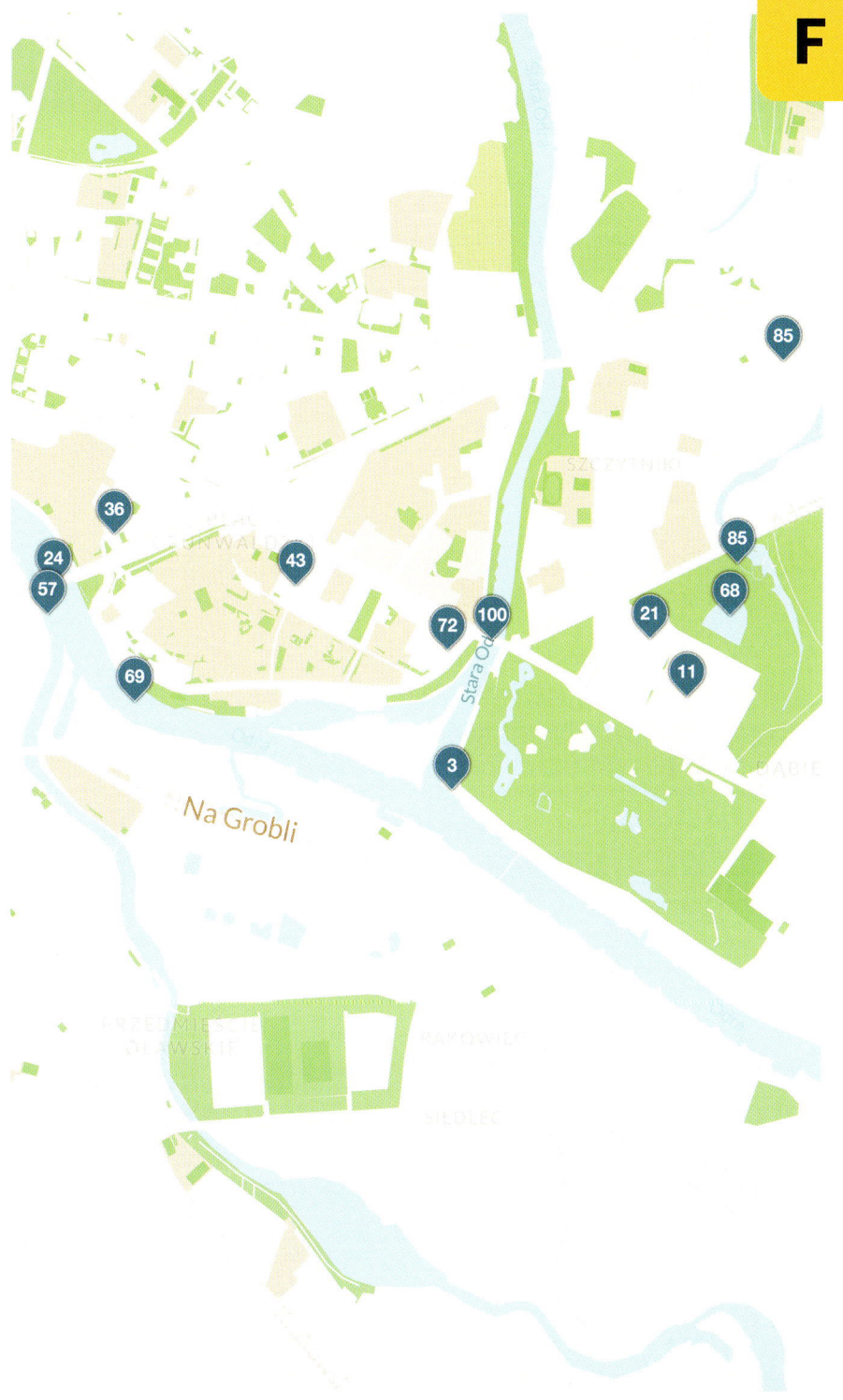

Picture credits

© Mirko Seebeck: All pictures unless otherwise mentioned in this section
© Ewa Kierach: p. 13, p. 79 (bottom), p. 96, p. 103, p. 129, p. 166 (top), p. 203 (bottom)
© Jerzy Wypych: p. 133 (top right and bottom)
© Małgorzata Kujda: p. 133 (top left)
© dpa/Kay Nietfeld: Picture of Hans Jörg Neumann on p. 216
© Marta Gutsche: Picture of Kasia on p. 228
© Alina Metelytsia: Picture of Jacek Sterczewski on p. 226

Maps: © Mapbox, © OpenStreetMap contributors and Aleksandra Gil. Prints use map data from Mapbox and OpenStreetMap and their data sources. To learn more, visit https://www.mapbox.com/about/maps/ and http://www.openstreetmap.org/copyright

Special thanks to Mr. Zenon for his approval to be shown in the picture on p. 43 with the mural. All additional pictures in the bonus chapter were provided by the individuals themselves.

Disclaimer

The research for this book was done based on the best knowledge and with the best intentions; however, mistakes can never be fully ruled out. Any hints, comments, and suggestions are more than welcome via email to info@wroclawguide.com

In particular, opening hours are subject to frequent changes, therefore, it is always advised to double-check the social media channels and web pages of the individual places.

If one of the places in this book is no longer operating, it will be exchanged in the next edition. But before you get a free replacement – we suggest subscribing to the WroclawGuide newsletter which will deliver the latest picks straight to your inbox.
Sign up at: https://wroclawguide.com/en/let-us-stay-in-touch

Big Thanks

First of all I'd like to express my thanks to all the people who shared their own three favourite places in Wrocław with the readers of this book. I was able to discover some great new places myself and am very thankful for that!

And, of course, I would like to thank Ewa for her tireless help and constant motivation. To Sarit for the great and patient advice on all sorts of book questions! To all the friends we have in Wrocław for their constant inspiration and love of discovery, which is really contagious. To the team of the Culture Train, which provided a lot of helpful contacts. Also to Johannes, who is infected by the Wrocław virus too and is constantly available with help, motivation, distractions, and anything else that is needed. To my parents, who certainly didn't always have it easy with me, but to whom I am very grateful that I can be around somewhere on this planet today. Then so much more credit goes out to the people who made this book so wonderful, starting with Christian, my editor for the English edition, who managed to de-Germanize all the phrases I wrote and did the final corrections. Nastia for the great cover and patience (do we let it glow or not?) and Ola for the great layout that makes everything look so much better. Also, it should not go unmentioned that most of the fonts used here come from Polish designers (Warsaw Types – Cyrulik by kroje.org and Lato by Łukasz Dziedzic).

Thanks, thanks, thanks!

I'd love to close out this book with a quote from Douglas Adams:

„I may not have gone where I intended to go,
but I think I have ended up where I needed to be."